The Meaning of
Work and Retirement

The Meaning of Work and Retirement

By

EUGENE A. FRIEDMANN

and

ROBERT J. HAVIGHURST

with

WILLIAM H. HARLAN

JANET BOWER

DOLORES C. GRUEN

RALPH R. IRELAND

ETHEL SHANAS

THE UNIVERSITY OF CHICAGO PRESS

THE UNIVERSITY OF CHICAGO PRESS, CHICAGO 37
Cambridge University Press, London, N.W. 1, England
The University of Toronto Press, Toronto 5, Canada

Preface

THIS book reports a set of studies of the significance of work in the lives of people and of the relations between the significance of work and attitudes toward retirement. It aims to lay a partial basis for a retirement policy that is both satisfactory to the individual and wise for the general welfare.

Parallel with these social-psychological studies has gone a study of flexible retirement practices in American business and industry.[1] This latter study was made in order to find out what was actually being done to fit retirement to the needs of the individual and to prepare people for retirement. It was found that a number of employers, large and small, have worked out retirement programs which enable the employee to continue working as long as he is productive and wishes to work. Thus a *flexible* retirement policy was shown to be practicable and successful in the experience of American business.

If a flexible retirement policy is practicable, there remains the question of when and under what circumstances a person should retire. This book is devoted to getting facts on the basis of which this question may be answered.

It has been pointed out by a number of sociologists that work has values other than purely financial ones in the lives of people. In 1949 the writer attempted to describe these extra-economic values or "meanings" of work and to show how the problem of retirement for the individual was related to the meanings of work for him. The writer's paper was presented at a meeting of the Gerontological Society in 1950 and later published as an appendix to a "University of Chicago Round Table" broadcast on the topic of retirement.[2]

1. Elizabeth Breckinridge, *Effective Use of Older Workers* (Chicago: Wilcox & Follett, 1953).

2. Robert J. Havighurst, "What It Means To Retire from Work," in *What about Retirement?* ("University of Chicago Round Table," No. 690, broadcast June 17, 1951), pp. 12–22.

During a research seminar on problems of old age in 1950 this topic was presented by the writer and then followed up by Eugene Friedmann, who gave it a better location in a framework of sociological theory. He and Ralph R. Ireland then carried out doctoral dissertations in 1950–51 based on study of the meanings of work and retirement for a group of skilled craftsmen.

At about this time the Rockefeller Foundation provided funds which enabled us to develop a more systematic set of studies, including people of widely different occupations and skill and education. These funds were used to support the study of steelworkers which was made by Mr. Friedmann in 1951–52 and to give minor assistance to those who made the studies of coalminers, salespeople, and physicians. Mr. Friedmann correlated the work of these people and worked out with them the plans for their contributions to this report.

The studies were supervised by the University of Chicago Committee for the Study of Later Maturity, which consisted at that time of Professor Ernest W. Burgess, Dr. Ethel Shanas, and the writer. Professor Burgess was active up to the time of his retirement in the planning of these studies. Dr. Shanas, as research directer for the committee, took part in the general planning and gave special assistance to Miss Bower and Mrs. Gruen in their studies.

In addition to the work of these people, it is a pleasure to acknowledge the interest and advice of Professors Philip Hauser and Everett C. Hughes and the assistance in the steelworker study of Charles Manley and James Singleton. The executives and personnel staff of the steel company, the department store, and the coal companies and the officers of the craftsmen's union all deserve our thanks, and their names are not given here because of the decision to keep these organizations anonymous.

ROBERT J. HAVIGHURST

CHICAGO, ILLINOIS
June 1953

Table of Contents

I

The Older Worker and the Meaning of Work

In the sweat of thy face shalt thou eat bread, till
thou return unto the ground.—GEN. 3:19.

W₈ LIVE in a time when work is changing its meaning in fundamental ways for people. Where work may formerly have been
motivated mainly by hunger or by desire for gain, this is no
longer the case.

THE CHANGING NECESSITY OF WORK

We now live in an economy which may become man's servant,
not his master. This economy we call an economy of abundance,
in contrast to the earlier economy of scarcity. When we have
solved the problem of producing enough goods to satisfy most
of the wants of men, we will still have before us the problem
of consuming these goods plentifully and wisely. We have
been blocked from this goal first by economic depression and
then by war; but, when we finally reach the goal, work will
no longer have the meaning of arduous exertion under the drive
of iron necessity which it had for so many societies from the
Garden of Eden to the twentieth century.

The time has already come when work need no longer be
a necessity for the whole of adult life. Within the current century a new social group has been added to the American population. These are the retired people, the people who are living
out the last ten or twenty years of their lives without working
for a living. In 1890 this group amounted to 31 per cent of the
male population over 65, or 1 per cent of the total male popula-

1

tion. In 1950 this group made up 58 per cent of the male population over 65, or 4 per cent of the total male population. There
was an even greater growth in numbers of retired women workers, though the actual number of women workers over 65 was
relatively small at both dates.

About one in five of the older people is living on an old age
pension from the government treasury. About one in four is
receiving old age insurance benefits under the federal Social
Security program. Under the present provisions of this program, three out of four people will eventually receive benefits.
Our society is attempting to provide an adequate economic
base for retirement of most people.

Thus retirement is not a rich man's luxury or an ill man's
misfortune. It is increasingly the common lot of all kinds of
people. Some find it a blessing; others, a curse. But it comes
anyway, whether blessing or curse, and it comes often in an
arbitrary manner, at a set age, without direct reference to the
productivity or the interest of the individual in his work.

THE SIGNIFICANCE OF WORK FOR THE INDIVIDUAL

As the process of retirement has been adding a new social
group to the life of our nation, so it has also been adding a new
period to the life-span of more and more workers. But, whereas
at least part of the cost of retirement to the nation can be calculated in terms of man-hours of productivity lost and non-
productive members added in our economy, the cost of retirement in the life of the individual is less readily perceived. By
retiring the worker, society takes from him his job and gives
him in exchange a subsidized period of life in which no work
activity is required. The young man's dream thus becomes the
old man's reality. But is it a fair exchange? To evaluate it
properly, we first must have some understanding of the part
the job has played in the total life-economy of the adult in our
society.

We know, of course, that the job fills a large portion of the
worker's time. As a matter of fact, there is no other waking
activity of the adult male in the United States which occupies
as great a portion of his life-span as does his job. In 1947, for

example, the working life-expectancy of the 20-year-old male was about forty-three years. He could look forward to spending more than 81,000 hours, or about 29 per cent, of his remaining waking life employed at a job.

However, the job is not only a time-filling activity. It is, more important, a purposeful activity which is expected of most adult males in our society. The job, or rather the productive system of which the job is a part, orients and controls the behavior of those persons who participate in it. It sets a goal for the worker, determines the manner in which the goal may be attained and the reward offered for its achievement, and affects the whole range of his participation in the society of which he is a member. Its influence extends even beyond the actual work life of the individual. If we could trace the life-history of the statistician's 20-year-old male referred to previously, we would find that a large portion of his pre-adult, pre-work life was spent in preparing for a job. We would also find that the part of his adult life not spent in work is, nonetheless, affected by whether or not he holds a job, the nature of the job he may hold, and the manner in which he performs it. In short, the job in our society exerts an influence which pervades the whole of the human life-span.

Thus, the job—or work activity—can be regarded as an axis along which the worker's pattern of life is organized. It serves to maintain him in his group, to regulate his life-activity, to fix his position in his society, and to determine the pattern of his social participation and the nature of his life-experiences and is a source of many of his satisfactions and affective experiences. In this sense, work can be said to perform certain *functions* in the life of the individual.

Certain of the functions of work are implied in the definition of the work "job" itself. The job gives the worker income or some form of economic return. This not only provides him with subsistence but also serves to maintain him at a certain level or "standard" of living which has been defined by his society. In exchange for income the job requires that he produce or contribute to the economy of the group. It takes from him a certain and usually a fixed amount of his time and effort and often requires that he be in a certain place of work. It determines to a large extent where, when, and how he is to spend a major part of his life. So the job has at least two functions: one of providing income or economic return, and the other of regulating the worker's pattern of life-activity.

Other functions of work are derived from the group context in which all jobs are set. A third function is the identification of the person in his group. The job is a description or a tag which marks the person, both at his place of employment and in the world outside. The tailor is so described in his shop. But he also might be thought of as a tailor by his family, his golf partners, his insurance agent, his minister, and other persons who enter into his nonwork life.

As the worker carries the identity of his job, so he also acquires the status which society has assigned to it. This status might be related to his particular type of employment, or it might be based merely on the fact that he holds a job. In either case job status is an important determinant of the individual's status in his family and community.

A fourth function which work performs is the fixing of patterns of association. Since work is always carried on in a group setting, the worker must relate in some fashion to the other members of his group. This may take place in the form of direct fact-to-face associations. Or it may occur in a more indirect manner where the other members of the group are not present but are represented in the form of audio-visual signals (i.e., buzzers, shouts, hand signals, lights, etc.), of written memos or directives, or merely of a set of unwritten group expectations. The association patterns of work also involve sets of subordinate-superordinate relationships. These can range from the simple "employer-employee" relation of the small shop or business to the complex pattern of relationships of the large corporation.

The fifth function of work is that of offering the worker a set of meaningful life-experiences. It is a source of contacts with persons, objects, and ideas. It is a market place where the worker's store of life-experience is enriched through interaction with the world about him and where he receives new ideas, expresses his own ideas, and modifies his conception of the world and of himself in relation to it.

The above five functions—income, regulating of life-activity, identification, association, and meaningful life-experience—are presented as general characteristics of work. They are to be found in any situation defined by society as a "job."[1]

WHAT WORK MEANS TO THE INDIVIDUAL

Although we have described work as having the same set of functions for all workers, we find that it does not have the same meaning for all individuals. We can gather this impression merely by listening to people talk about their jobs—the insurance salesman telling about his troubles and excitement in "cracking" a tough customer, the executive describing the responsibilities and worries of his job, the assembly-line worker complaining about the monotony of his job yet bragging that he is the best worker in the plant. Meanings vary as jobs vary and as people vary. Yet there are some common threads which run through the diversity.

The significance of the job, as interpreted by the worker himself, can be regarded as varying in two fundamental ways. First, it differs according to the particular recognition the person has made of the part which the job has played in his life. Certainly, we can expect that in our culture practically all workers recognize their job as a way of earning a living. However, we may also discover that many individuals have come to recognize other functions of the job as well. For example, some may view it in terms of the prestige (or lack of prestige) it gives them in the community; for others it may be the chief source of contact they have with the outside world, or it may be regarded as the locus of association with friends and fellow-workers. The recognitions

1. This analysis of the functions of work in our society is in general accord with Linton's concept of *function* (Ralph Linton, *The Study of Man* [New York: Appleton-Century Co., 1936], chap. xxiii). The function of an element of culture may be thought of as the contribution which it makes toward the satisfaction of needs of people. Merton has added to this concept by distinguishing between "manifest" and "latent" functions (Robert K. Merton, *Social Theory and Social Structure* [Glencoe, Ill.: Free Press, 1949], chap. i). Some of the functions of work mentioned above are latent functions; that is, they contribute to the satisfaction of people's needs without being recognized by people generally.

made of the functions of work, therefore, would vary according to the individual's conception of the part which the job has played in his life.

Second, the individual's interpretation of the job experience varies according to the type of evaluation he makes of his work. Around all the work functions cluster a variety of emotional experiences. From the job the worker derives such feelings as success, failure, accomplishment, frustration, good fellowship, aesthetic pleasure, and boredom. Thus work may be welcomed by him as a joy or dreaded as a burden.

In speaking of the meanings of work, then, we are speaking both of the individual's recognition of the part the job has played in his life and of the type of affective response he has made to it. It would be hard to conceive of a neutral recognition of work function without any feeling tone attached to it.[2]

Table 1 presents an illustrative list of some of the meanings which the individual may assign to his job and shows how they may be related to the more universal functions of work.

STUDYING THE MEANINGS OF WORK

In this research we have studied the positive meanings that people in several different occupations find in their work. We have studied people who were past 55 (with the exception of one study) because we are interested in the problem of retirement and because we want to find out how job satisfactions are related in the worker's mind to the question of his retirement when retirement has already come or is clearly visible. We assume that retirement will bring or has brought a loss of certain satisfactions and thus create a void in a person's life which he will seek somehow to fill.

Our initial investigation (the study of skilled craftsmen discussed in chap. v) considered the members of a single occupational group. We wanted to determine (*a*) whether work had

2. In making this distinction between *meanings* and *functions* of work, we are following both Linton (*op cit.*) and Merton (*op cit.*). These writers stress the usefulness of distinguishing between the objective significance (the function) of a culture element in making the culture meet the needs of people and the subjective significance (the meaning) of this element to the individual. We are studying meanings and thus incidentally throwing light on the functions of work in our culture.

meanings for members of this group in addition to that of earning a living and (*b*) whether those persons who emphasize the extra-economic meanings of work would regard retirement less favorably than those persons who viewed work as primarily a way of earning a living. We found that members of this group did indeed stress meanings of work other than earning a living and that a relationship could be demonstrated between the mean-

TABLE 1

THE RELATION BETWEEN THE FUNCTIONS AND MEANINGS OF WORK

Work Function	Work Meaning
1. Income	*a*) Maintaining a minimum sustenance level of existence
	b) Achieving some higher level or group standard
2. Expenditure of time and energy	*a*) Something to do
	b) A way of filling the day or passing time
3 Identification and status	*a*) Source of self-respect
	b) Way of achieving recognition or respect from others
	c) Definition of role
4. Association	*a*) Friendship relations
	b) Peer-group relations
	c) Subordinate-superordinate relations
5. Source of meaningful life-experience	*a*) Gives purpose to life
	b) Creativity; self-expression
	c) New experience
	d) Service to others

ings assigned to work and the individual's attitude toward retirement.

We then applied our approach to other occupational and skill groups in an attempt to extend our knowledge of the meaning of work and to see how they vary not only among individuals of the same group but also between groups of different skill and occupation levels. Our hypotheses for the study were as follows:

1. Work has recognized meanings in addition to that of earning a living.
2. Those persons who regard work as primarily a way of earning a living will prefer to retire at age 65 (or normal retirement age).
3. Those persons who stress values of work other than that of earning a living will prefer to continue working past age 65.

4. The extra-economic meanings of work are stressed to a greater extent by members of the higher skilled occupational groups.

IMPLICATIONS FOR THE OLDER WORKER

An understanding of the significance of work in the life of the adult in our society has several implications for the consideration of the adjustment problem of the older worker. First, it can be useful in deciding the question of who shall retire. It might be expected that persons who regard work as only a way of earning a living would welcome retirement at the earliest age at which they could get an adequate retirement income. Conversely, those persons for whom work has been more than just a way of earning a living may prefer to work as long as they are physically able to do the job. Premature retirement at an arbitrarily set age could represent a major and sudden disruption of their pattern of life and make the adjustment to old age much more difficult for them.

Second, it can contribute to the understanding of the adjustment process involved in retirement. If work has played an important part in the life of the individual, then the process of adjustment to retirement is a twofold one. The worker must adjust both to the *entering* of a new situation and to the *leaving* of an old situation and the loss of the values it has had throughout much of his adult life.

Third, it is an important consideration in selecting activities suitable for retired persons. For example, a man whose work life has been a mixture of responsibility, recognition, worry, aspiration, and hope might find basket-weaving or leatherworking, fishing or even gardening, a rather poor substitute for the meaningful activity of his adult life. Merely finding activity or hobbies to fill the leisure time of the retired person is not enough. These activities should offer satisfactions to replace those which the worker received as an active, productive member of society.

THE PLAN OF THE STUDIES

The several studies reported in the following chapters all had a common interest in the meanings of work and the relations of these meanings to problems of retirement. They were all aimed at testing the hypotheses stated in this chapter. Yet they were made by five different people over a period of about two years; and each person worked with a considerable degree of autonomy. Each study was to a considerable extent exploratory, thus serving to modify the concepts and procedures of those which followed it. One result of this is that the results of the several studies are not strictly comparable. To have insisted upon making them so either would have placed the later studies in a strait jacket or would have required the repetition of the earlier studies with all the improvements made in the later ones.

Still, some comparison of the results in five different occupational groups is possible, and this comparison (chap. viii) provides some of the most interesting and significant results of the research.

II

The Meanings of Work and Retirement for Steelworkers

O<small>UR</small> initial investigation of the meanings of work, a mail questionnaire study of a group of skilled craftsmen, indicated that work had meanings in addition to that of earning a living and that the meanings the worker derived from his job were related to his attitude toward retirement.[1] These workers, however, were artisans of a skill and income level well above that of the average American workman. What, then, of the less-skilled industrial worker who is supposed to be typical of twentieth-century Western society? Is earning a living the only meaning he attaches to his job—the only satisfaction he derives from it? Is work a drudgery for him and retirement a welcome relief, or is he still reluctant to leave his job even when he has achieved some degree of the economic security prized in his society?

To extend our knowledge of the meaning of work and to test our hypotheses concerning differences in meaning of various skill levels, a group of unskilled and semiskilled workers in a basic heavy industry—steel—was selected for study. In general, we felt that (1) members of this semi- and unskilled group of workers would stress a way of earning a living as the primary meaning of work for them; (2) most members would prefer to retire at age 65; and (3) given an adequate retirement income, most members of this group would report satisfaction with retirement.

THE GROUP STUDIED

The co-operation of the company and union officials of a large midwestern steel mill was obtained. The study universe was

1. See below, chap. v.

composed of all "white," male, unskilled and semiskilled[2] workers, 55 years and older, who were employed at the company or who had been retired within the last five years.[3] About 15 per cent of the employed and retired workers 55 and over were Negro and Mexican. It was decided to eliminate these so-called "nonwhite" workers from the study, since the job opportunities available to them and their life-patterns were somewhat different from those of other workers at this skill level.

The workers included in the study can be divided into three subgroups on the basis of age and employment status. First is the group of employed workers in the 55–64 age group. Second is a very small group of men who have reached their sixty-fifth birthday since November, 1949, and have elected to remain at their jobs. Third is the group of men who have retired since the company adopted the age 65 retirement practice in 1946. This last group includes those men who were required to retire prior to November, 1949, and those who, since that date, either asked to retire at age 65 or were unable to meet the company's physical requirements for continuing at their regular jobs (Table 2).

STUDY PROCEDURE

Since the literacy level of this group of steelworkers was low, the use of a written questionnaire was not feasible. Moreover, it was felt that a more flexible and intensive investigation technique—such as the interview—would increase our understanding

2. The distinction between the higher skilled workers and the semi- and unskilled groups was made in a rather arbitrary manner. The company has divided its hourly rated mill jobs into thirty-four categories on a pay scale which increases progressively from categories 1 to 34. The various job categories are assigned numbers on the basis of the amount of skill and training required, job hazards, strenuousness, desirability, and certain other considerations associated with each particular job. Upon consultation with one of the company's industrial engineers, it was decided that all men in job categories 1 through 12 could probably be considered unskilled or semiskilled workers as defined by the *Dictionary of Occupational Titles*. Whereas it is possible that some semiskilled workers may carry a rating higher than 12, our consultant felt that the number of exceptions would be small. He also indicated that the inclusion of job categories higher than 12 would introduce a large number of skilled workers.

3. The company, which will be called "Caltown Steel," first instituted the practice of retiring men at age 65 in April, 1946. This practice was discontinued in November, 1949.

of the basic "meaning-of-work" concept. The question, then, was how to conduct an interview which would test the study hypotheses.

Certain difficulties in interviewing this group were apparent, but these proved to be greater in anticipation than they were in actuality. First, there was the problem of language difficulty. Most of the group were foreign-born, and many of them had a poor command of English. Although the interviewers neither spoke nor understood the foreign languages native to the subjects, it was found that with patience a fairly satisfactory interview could be conducted in English in most cases. In those few

TABLE 2

STUDY UNIVERSE: "WHITE," MALE, RE-
TIRED AND EMPLOYED, UNSKILLED
AND SEMISKILLED WORKERS, 55 YEARS
AND OVER

Subgroup	No.
Employed, 55–64 years	833
Employed, 65 and over	21
Retired	150
Total	1,004

cases where the subject understood little or no English, a willing interpreter was always found in the form of a relative, neighbor, friend, bartender, or other interested person.

The next problem visualized was that of obtaining the subject's co-operation. This group is not generally considered to be "interview-minded," and it was thought that the public opinion poll might be strange to them. Further, since part of the interview dealt with retirement practices and pension payments—once a contested issue between the company and the union—there was a question as to how the interviewer should represent himself so as to minimize the subject's suspicion and hostility. Although both the company and the union furnished the interviewers with letters of introduction, it was found that representing this study as a university survey was usually the only introduction needed. To the interviewers' surprise, many of these persons welcomed and even seemed flattered by the notion that their opinions were wanted. Others who thought the interview procedure pointless or were openly suspicious of the interviewers' motives were, nevertheless, usually willing to hear them out and gave at least qualified answers to the questions asked. In many of these cases the subjects' hostility and doubts seemed to diminish as the interview progressed.

The interview procedure developed in the course of the pre-test centered around certain areas of life-experience. The subject was encouraged to talk about his experiences and feelings, and the interviewer tried to follow the subject's lead in structuring the interview rather than following any schedule of questions to be asked. The interview plan, then, varied with the subject. But, in general, the subject was encouraged to do the following:

1. Describe his present (or last) job
   a) What does he do and how does he do it?
   b) How does he like it? Why or why not? And, more specifically, what does he like and dislike about it?
   c) What does (or will) he miss about it upon retirement?
2. Contrast this with other jobs he has had
   a) What other jobs has he held (work history)?
      What were they like? How did he get into them?
   b) How does this job compare with others?
   c) Of the jobs he has had, which has he liked best or least? Why?
   d) If he had his life to live over again, what sort of work would he want to go into?
   e) If he were asked to advise a young fellow today on a line of work to go into, what would he suggest?
3. Discuss his retirement plans and attitudes
   a) Does he intend (or did he want) to retire at age 65? Why or why not?
   b) How does he feel about retirement?
   c) At what age and under what circumstances does he think a man ought to retire?
   d) If employed, what concerns him about retirement?
   e) If retired, what problems has he met? How has he tried to solve them?
4. Supply the interviewer with the following information:
   a) Economic data: What sources of income will (or does) he have upon retirement? How much does it amount to? How adequate is it? Does he own his home?
   b) Living arrangements: Where and with whom is he living?
   c) Marital and family status

d) Activities: If employed, what does he do in his spare time? Which of these activities will he continue after retirement? If retired, how does he fiill his day? Has he looked for a job?

e) Other personal data: Age, nativity, etc.

This outline gives a topic guide of the interview process, but the order and manner in which the information was elicited was left up to the interviewer himself. Two experienced interviewers were used, both thoroughly familiar with the study's frame of reference and the hypotheses which were being tested. They were given leeway to probe as deeply as they were able, to digress onto related but possibly irrelevant topics, and to explore the limits of the study's framework to whatever extent they could. Notes were not taken during the interview, but the interviewer recorded it almost immediately afterward. Although we cannot claim to have made verbatim transcriptions, we feel that after an initial practice period we were able to produce a record that was accurate as to both factual content and flavor of speech.

The question of the meanings which work had for the individual was considered too abstract to be asked directly. The interviewer, therefore, had to infer the meanings from the manner in which the subject viewed the jobs he held and his indicated likes and dislikes. Since the inferring of meanings is a subjective process, it was decided to attempt a reliability check. One-third of the interviews were conducted jointly, and both interviewers collaborated on the writeup. After the writeup was completed, each interviewer independently rated the meanings of work for the subject. A comparison of the ratings showed that the two interviewers agreed in the categories of meaning they assigned in 96 per cent of the cases.

THE SAMPLE SELECTED

We wanted to study the experiences and attitudes of men just prior to the age of retirement and compare them with those of men who had already retired. We interviewed sixty employed men 55–64 years of age, fifty men 65 and older, and eighteen men 65 years and over who had remained at their jobs (see Tables 3 and 4).[4]

The group of 128 respondents ranged in age from 55 to 81 years. Eighty per cent of them were foreign-born, mainly of Central and Eastern European origin. The educational level of the group was low. About 95 per cent had no more than eight

TABLE 3

THE GROUP STUDIED

Status	Total No.	Sample Size	No. of Respondents	Per Cent of Response
Employed, 55–64.............	833	67	60	90
Employed, 65 and over.......	19	19	18	95
Retired....................	150	52	50	94
Total..................	1,002	138	128	93

TABLE 4

AGE DISTRIBUTION OF RESPONDENTS

Age	Employed	Retired	
55–59.........	29	....	
60–64.........	31	....	Retirement Age
65–69.........	17	27	
70–74.........	1*	15	
75–79.........	....	6	
80 and over....	....	2	
Total......	78	50	

*Since men were allowed to continue working past 65 only after November, 1949, the maximum age of any presently employed man should be 68. However, in this case, the respondent claimed that the plant records did not list his correct age.

4. A random sample of the employed men in the 55–64 year age range was drawn, and the group was contacted without replacement until a total of 60 interviews were obtained; 7 refusals were encountered in the process, bringing the sample total up to 67. A systematic sample of the retired men was drawn, and a similar procedure followed until a total of 50 interviews were achieved; 2 refusals give a sample total of 52 for the group. As there were only 19 employed men in the 65-year-and-over age range, the entire group was included in the study; 18 completed interviews and 1 refusal were obtained. A total stratified sample of 138, representing 14 per cent of the universe, was drawn. Interviews were obtained from 128 members, or 93 per cent of the sample.

grades of schooling, many having had little or no formal schooling. In general, they were family men. Fifty-five per cent were
married and living with their wives, and only 14 per cent had
never been married. Seventy-three per cent lived in the industrial city in which the mill was located, and the rest resided
in various other industrial cities surrounding the plant. Forty-
four per cent of them owned their homes. Eighty-six per cent
of the men had been employed at the plant for sixteen years or
longer, and almost 30 per cent had worked there over twenty-
five years.

HOW THEY BECAME STEELWORKERS

Unlike the present-day American youth, who is encouraged
to select a career according to his interests and abilities, it is
doubtful that, when these men were young, many of them
ever expected to spend the major part of their working life in
a steel mill. Work—finding a job—was a necessity for most of
them, often while they were still in their early teens. If a
job could not be found in one place, they moved to another, and
the jobs they took were usually more a matter of availability
than of choice. This is particularly apparent among the immigrant workers of this group. They came because they were
attracted by the prospect of jobs at good wages, to escape conditions in their native land, or for other reasons. They came
with varying hopes and expectations. But only a handful came
because they wanted to work in a steel mill.

The Immigrant Worker

Many of the foreign-born workers in the mills came to this
country, as in the following example, with the intention of earning some money and then returning [hooker, age 56]:

Q. Why did you come to America?
A. Well, I tell you. We were poor farmers like most people over
there. We did not have much land, and I was the youngest son. I heard
that they paid lots of money in America; so I came. I thought I would
stay a little while, save some money, then go back and buy a farm. I
got a job as soon as I came over here. They paid $1.25 for ten hours'
work. That was good pay for those days. Pretty soon I got $1.60 a day.
I figured that, if I could make money like that over here, why should I

go back and struggle over there for a living, like my father had to do. So I stayed. Then I got married, and I was stuck here for good. (*Laughs*.)

Others came intending to stay. They came because there were no jobs for them in their native country [general laborer, age 66]:

Q. What country did you come from, Mr. G.?
A. From Lithuania. It used to be Russia, but in 1920 it was made a free country.
Q. What job did you do over there?
A. All they had were farms in Lithuania. (Wife agrees.) They only had two factories, a whiskey factory and a lumber mill. Everything else was farms. I worked on a farm till I came to this country. I didn't like to work on a farm. I went into the Russian army for four years, and after I got out I came to this country in 1913. In 1918 I brought my wife and children over. I came right to Michigan City and worked in the car company.

Some came to avoid serving in the army [hooker, age 61]:

Q. How did you happen to come here, Mr. K.?
A. I came over to this country in 1912.
Bartender: Make him tell you how he came over! He did it to escape going in the Turkish army!
Mr. K.: That's right. I was a Greek, but I was living in Macedonia, under Turkish rule. They started a war against Greece and were going to draft me to fight against my own people. I just ran away. I traveled at night and escaped the country and came over here.

And one man came in search of romance [retired, age 80]:

Q. You say you came from Germany, Mr. B.?
A. Yes, I was a harness-maker there. I was an apprentice for four years. Then I went from town to town doing work. I went all over Germany with a gang of men working from one place to another. One time we came to Danzig. (Here Mr. B. hummed a little tune and murmured, "Ein tausend zwasig—gute alte Danzig.") I went to a dance hall one night. I met a pretty girl there who was a good dancer. I danced with her all night. I asked her to meet me the next night. She said she couldn't; she was going to America. I asked her to wait for one month so I could save some money and come to America with her. She was the best dancer I ever met. She waited for me, and I came to the United States. When we got to New York, her family wanted to know when we were getting married. I didn't want to marry her, but she started to cry. So I went down one day and we got married on paper.

Many regarded America as a land of opportunity, as a goal worth striving for [retired, age 65]:

I came here from Europe, from what was Hungary. But the borders were changed after the first World War, and it was part of Czechoslovakia. My son's godfather had come over here and was working at a steel mill. He wrote back that there were good jobs. So I came over. I had to go into the army for two years in 1906. I got married in 1909 and had a son in 1910. Then I told my wife I wanted to go to America. She did not want me to go, but I did anyway. I could not get passport papers from the government. They said I was to go back into the army in 1911. But four friends of mine went with me, and we walked nine days and nine nights across to the German border. Then we applied for passports and got them right away. We came to this country and never had any trouble. My wife came over then in 1913 with my son.

But one man arrived here by mistake [bolt-cutter, age 66]:

Q. How did you come to this country?
A. I was sailing. I sailed betwen Europe and America for six years on the Cunard Lines. I even got to Chicago. One night in New York the captain and I got into an argument, and I got kicked off. So I was in America. I had no intention of staying in this country, but I never did get back to Europe.

Once here, they sought work in the industrial areas of the East and the Midwest, although one nationality group, the Greeks, first went out West to work on the railroads. They entered the occupational structure at the bottom, taking whatever unskilled jobs there were available to "foreigners" at that time. They switched from job to job at first, either being laid off or else looking for work that was less backbreaking or that offered better pay. But mostly they found that, for men who did not speak English, only the heaviest and dirtiest jobs in the unskilled labor market could be had.

Some, as in the following case, were embittered and disillusioned by their experiences [retired, age 65]:

Q. What kind of work did you do?
A. Oh, I did all kinds of work; labor work mostly, heavy hard work. I came over to this country in 1906. I landed in New Orleans. I went to work in a sugar-cane field there. They paid me 65 cents a day for fourteen hours' work. I had a Spanish and a Negro foreman. We were just foreigners to them, and they treated us like that mostly. The work was hard, and they would swear at us. All the time, my foreman would

call me a son-of-a-bitch. He would say, "Come here, you son-of-a-bitch."
I did not know English; I did not know what it meant. But I could speak
a little German. So one day I asked an Austrian man, who was working
with me, what means "son-of-a-bitch." He said, "A bitch is a dog."
Next time the foreman me called that, I asked him why. He said he
called everybody that. I said, "You called me the son of a dog. That
means my mother was a dog. My mother was not a dog." I told him,
"She was a woman, just like your mother." He said, "God damn you."
I say, "You don't say that. God, he lives upstairs. You live down here.
You don't say that." He got very angry, and I quit. Then I went to
work for the railroad up in Mississippi. I carried ties. It was heavy work,
but it was a much better job. They paid me $1.25 for twelve hours'
work. Then from there I went up to Detroit. I did labor work in Detroit.
Then I went to a rubber factory in Ohio. I moved about quite a bit.
But everywhere I went I was just a foreigner. They did not care much
about foreigners. Then I went to work in Chicago. I went to work at
the Stock Yards. I worked there a while; then I went up to Milwaukee.
Then I came back to Chicago. Then I went to work in a foundry in
Caltown. I worked as a hooker. Then I went to work for the Lakeport
Cement Company. I stayed there for eleven years, up until 1932. I oper-
ated a crane there.

Q. Which job did you like best?

A. Oh, they were all hard work; nobody cared much about you. I
worked at the Lakeport Cement Company until 1932. Then they shut
down the section in which I was working. I could not find a job for
one and a half years, and I went on relief. Then, in 1933, when Roosevelt
came in, and they had the NRA, Caltown Steel opened a plant. They
called for men, and I went over there, and they gave me a janitor job.

A few tried to rise above the unskilled level but failed [scarfer,
age 59]:

Q. How did you happen to come to Caltown?

A. You want the story of my life? I'll tell you. I started to work on
the railroads out West, out around Montana and Idaho. That was in 1912,
1913, and 1914. Things were pretty bad then, not like now. We worked
like animals. If the foreman saw somebody resting for a minute, he
was out on them, pushing them along. I moved around a lot then, looking
for steady work. I heard there was work in Chicago. At the Stock Yards
I heard they put men on around Christmas time. I did not know anything
about that work, about animals or butchering. But it was close to Christmas, and I wanted some work. I went out there. They let me work a
couple of hours the first day, a couple of hours the second day, and a
couple of hours a third day. Then they told me there was no more work;
we could go home. Do you know what my check was for that work?

I never forget it. For three days' work, a few hours each day, I got a check of $1.65. In those days you did not ask how much a job paid; you just asked for work. Then I heard of the Metropolis mill; they were hiring men out there. So I went out there and got a job for a while. But I did not like the work.

Q. What job did you have?

A. Oh, just labor work in the mill. It was heavy work, and it was hot and dirty too. It was not steady work either. So I came over to Caltown in 1916. Some of the men told me it was a good place to work, and they were just expanding the plant then. I worked here till 1918 and came back in 1920.

Q. What did you do in those two years when you left Caltown Steel?

A. (*Gives an embarrassed laugh.*) Well, you want to hear a story? I tell you another story. I tell you the honest truth. I became a business-man. I opened up a little dry-cleaning shop down the street. But I went out of business in a couple of years. I was just another little businessman that failed.

Q. Why did you go out of business?

A. I found that I was not making any more money than I did with Caltown Steel, and I had to work much longer hours. I worked all day, and then I had to stay open three or four nights a week, Sundays and holidays, too. It was not like now when you close your shop when you like. Business was hard to get then, and you had to have your shop open almost all the time.

Q. Why did you go into business for yourself?

A. I wanted to get steady work, steady income. We would only get two or three days' work a week at Caltown Steel then. And if a man has a family just growing up, he wants steady work, steady pay, do you understand?

And some found an escape in drink [retired, age 69]:

Q. How did you happen to get started at Caltown Steel?

A. Oh, I worked there three or four times since I came to this country. I was young then and liked to try different jobs. Young men today are like that. They go from one job to the next. They won't stay on dirty, hard jobs. They quit. I did not have any schooling and could not read or write. So I had to take the dirty labor jobs. I came to this country in 1906. I worked a while in Pennsylvania on the railroad and then came here to the mill. I worked on the furnace when they had one plant. Then in 1919 I was working on a job where the boss was bad. He was dirty; he chewed tobacco and drank on the job and gave his friends the good jobs. I did not like that, and I told him so. He said, "You don't like it—quit!" I quit that job, and my brother got me a job at Caltown Steel. Then I got sick. I was sick for fourteen months. One doctor said I had lung trouble; another said I had sinus trouble; another said I had diabetes; another said I had goiter. I weighed 185 pounds before I got sick and went down to 115 pounds. Then a friend of mine told me to start drinking wine. Right away I felt better, and in two months I was well again.

But, after a period of searching and trying, most of the immigrant workers settled down to the tasks of everyday living—of supporting themselves and their families. They made peace with the society that assigned jobs with little regard for individual ability or preference. They raised their families, bought homes, and, in general, adapted themselves to the life of a steelworker.

The Native-born Steelworker

In a sense the career line of some of the native-born workers paralleled that of the immigrant. These were persons who came from rural areas, where there was little economic opportunity, to the industrial areas of the city. The steel mill represented their first step into industrial society. Some found the work to their liking and remained [pump-station engineer, age 59]:

Q. What did you do before you came to Caltown?

A. I was a farmer down South, in the Deep South, down in Tennessee. I was a cotton farmer; but the boll weevils got so bad I just could not make a living on it. I had family trouble; my wife went one way, and I went the other. I came up here in 1924 and stayed ever since.

Q. Did you own your own farm in Tennessee?

A. No, I was a renter. The place I was on was a plantation of 17,000 acres. The owners were making a go of it, too. Just the year after I left, they started using poison on the boll weevils. They'd keep the place in good shape. After four years of cotton, they'd move us somewhere else and let the land rest.

Q. Did you like farming?

A. Yes, that's a good life. If you are sick or want to rest a day or two, the things you planted keep growing. They don't stop just because you are sick for a day. It's not like here at the plant. You have to punch a time clock every day, or you do not have anything coming in.

Q. How did you hear about Caltown Steel?

A. Oh, there are a lot of people here from the South. You'd be surprised. I just came North and heard about it from friends of mine.

Q. Are you glad you started to work there?

A. I'll tell you: You may be surprised, but I've never gone past the fourth grade in school. I worked my way up to this job all on my own. I learned everything on the job. When I came to Caltown Steel, I took one look at the electric lights they had burning. I said to myself, "as long as this place is going, they'll need someone to keep these lights running." So I took a job as sweeper in the power plant and worked my way up. A lot of men laughed at me. I could have gotten a little more money by working in the mill. But when the depression hit, the men in the mill were laid off. I was part-time engineer as well as oiler then. They had to let some men go, and I was put back on full-time oiler. But I never worked less than five days a week all during the depression. Of course, I only made $3.00 for eight hours, but I always had something coming in. The men that had laughed at me came around later; they said, "We used to laugh at you for not taking a job in the mill for more money. But you were right. We got laid off, and you were still working." I was content to work up in the pump house. I did not want all the money so long as I always had a job.

A few, seeking opportunities not available to them in semi-skilled work, used their jobs both as a springboard from which they could move up the economic ladder and as a reserve "trade" which they could fall back on if they failed. Others drifted from job to job, without purpose or direction, working always at the unskilled labor jobs of society.

To the extent that they were newcomers to an industrial society and were forced to enter at the bottom of the occupational structure, the careers of these men were similar to that of the immigrant worker. Being native-born, however, their progress seemed to be somewhat easier than that of the immigrant. In general, jobs were easier to find for them, and a choice was available within the unskilled and semiskilled range. Having no language barrier, they probably were more proficient in their dealings with hiring agents and foremen and thus were able to avoid the heaviest and the dirtiest of the industrial jobs.

Included in the group of native-born was the popular prototype of the industrial worker in Western society—the men who were born and reared in industrial areas, who found their earliest job opportunities in the mills[5] [retired, age 66]:

5. This group of men was small, however, amounting to less than 5 per cent of the foreign-born in the sample and about 40 per cent of the native-born; over 90 per cent of the group studied were not born in industrial areas but migrated to them.

Q. Have you always worked around this area?

A. Yes, I was born in South Chicago. I always worked hard. I was a big, husky kid. I was never afraid of anything. Sometimes when I needed money for a week end, I'd go to work in a warehouse and sling freight. You know, when I was seventeen, I went over to a steel mill and got a job. I saw that the hookers were making pretty good pay. I talked the foreman into letting me try it. That was a rough job in those days. The hooker lifted the hot billets with a pair of tongs. They did not have a crane then. The foreman told me that I was a crazy kid, that it was man's work. But I insisted, and he said, "Go ahead and try it if you want to." So I tried it. I caught on in a hurry. The foreman saw I was doing okay, so he let me stay at it. Then, one day, the superintendent came through and saw what I was doing. He called me over and said, "Young fellow, that's not a job for you. You're just a kid. Why, in ten years you'd be dead if you did that sort of work. You go back to your old job; and when you get to be a man, say, thirty or thirty-five, you come back and see me, and I'll get you a job as a hooker if you are still interested."

Q. What other sorts of jobs have you held?

A. Oh, I could keep you here all day telling you all the jobs I've worked at. I was a pipe-fitter over in Caltown Steel. That was in 1919. But I only stayed there a few weeks. They had a strike. The company wanted me to keep on working, but I told them I wouldn't cross the picket lines. I didn't go out on the picket line; I just quit. I didn't want to stay on at a plant like that. So I went out and got a job at a foundry in South Chicago. I painted smoke stacks. I used to climb 200-foot stacks and paint the top. I liked that job. I bet I could climb that stack right now if you wanted to dare me. (*Pauses.*) I wouldn't do it unless you dared me, though. That's a young man's job. (*Laughs.*) Then I did other sorts of work, too. I operated the big unloading crane at the dock in the Calumet River here, and I did many other things. But I never liked to stay on a job too long.

Q. What would you say was the best job you ever had?

A. Now that's a tough one; I don't know. I suppose my job at Caltown Steel was the best for an old man; it was steady, and the pay was good. Then, I had a good gang of men to work with; we had a lot of fun. I knew I was getting older, and I figured I'd better stay in one place and put something aside so I could quit working when I would be an old man. But I don't think I would have stayed on there if I were young.

Q. Why not?

A. I never liked to stay on one job too long; I never was afraid of work. Besides, I had a knack of getting along with people wherever I went. So it was always easy for me to find a new job.

Q. Why did you want to change jobs so often?

A. I was young then, liked to shift around a bit, looked for jobs that paid more money.

Q. You wanted a better-paying job, then?

A. Yes. I guess so. But that wasn't really all I wanted. I'd like new jobs. Each job is something different; new people to meet, new things to do. I looked forward to them.

Q. You certainly had a lot of work experience in your life. Tell me, if you had your life to live over again, if you could be a young man again, what sort of work would you want to do?

A. (*Thinks a minute and then grins as he answers.*) You know, I'd do the same things all over again. I sort of liked the jobs I did.

Q. Are there any jobs you didn't work at that you might want to try if you could do it again?

A. I don't know; there might be. But the important thing to me was working till I got tired of the job and then finding something new. The only reason I stayed at Caltown Steel as long as I did was because I felt I was getting too old to shift jobs like I used to.

These men were products of an industrial environment and were able to handle a wide variety of mill jobs; almost all of them had at one time advanced to the skilled-job level. However, they ended their work careers at the unskilled or semi-skilled level either because they were physically unable to do their former jobs or were downgraded as a result of the elimination of their previous jobs through technological change or because they left the mills for other enterprises and then returned.

THE STEELWORKER'S VIEW OF HIS JOB

In considering the work histories of these men and their own reflections on their careers, one fact stands out: If they could have acted as free agents in their environments and selected the jobs at which they were to work, few would have chosen the job in steel they held for most of their adult lives. When asked, "If you could have your life to live over again and could choose any line of work you liked, what job would you want?"[6] only 18 per cent selected their present job or one similar to it. Even more revealing is their suggestion for a person who would have a greater freedom of choice than they had, when asked, "What

6. An approximate form of the actual question used. The phrasing in each case was left to the interviewer to work out in the course of the interview.

sort of job would you advise a young fellow today to try to get?" only 8 per cent suggested a job in steel at their level.

There was a variety of opinions as to the jobs they would have taken. Forty-two per cent would have gone into steel again, but most of them would have wanted a higher-rated job than the one they had. Only 28 per cent would advise a young man to go into steel today, however, and, again, most of them suggested a job level higher than their own. Those who specified jobs outside of steel stressed the skilled trades. Having a skill meant steady pay to them—a job without seasonal layoffs. It also meant "easy" work—work which required knowledge and ability but was not the heavy labor of their jobs in the mill. Similarly education was a way of achieving the "better" jobs [millwright's helper, age 58]:

Q. What do you think are the best jobs at Caltown Steel?

A. The best jobs are where you to use your brains—you get paid for using your brains. Anyone can get a job where you only need muscle, but you never get good money for being strong. Roller is really the best job at a steel plant—you have to use your head for that. Next, I think electrician is a good job, and after that mechanic. If you've got brains (*taps forehead*), you can do good in those jobs.

Friend: You want to know something? Excuse me for interrupting, but I can tell you something that's a fact. Weak men get the hardest jobs. Strong men get easy jobs. I'll prove it to you: Go through any big plant. All you see is little guys like me lifting things three times as big as they are. The big men are all operating machines or they're foremen or have some easy job. That's a fact.

Q. If you would be young again and have your life to live all over again, what sort of work would you want to do?

A. I'd go to school if I were young again. I'd go to a business college and learn a job that takes brains. I'd want to use my mind—it's the men who do that that do some good in this world. Most men can't think—they'll do a job the same way all their lives—even if it's backward from the way it should be done. If you use your mind, though, you can make jobs easier and get them done better. I know a man who got a job putting screws through parts of machines. They way it was, the screws would break every day or so, and they always needed fixing. He wasn't doing that for a week till he told them how to fix the machine so the screws would never break. All they had to do was drill another hole and fasten it differently. That's what I mean about using your mind. If you get that kind of job, you can improve things—really make jobs better. You don't have to go to college to do that—even a mechanic can do it if he's got brains. If I couldn't go to school, I'd be a mechanic—that can be a good job.

Twenty-one per cent stated that they would get an education if they had it to do over again, and 30 per cent offered that advice to a young fellow starting out today. An education in this case did not refer to a specific course of training for any particular profession or occupation. Rather it seemed to be the key to moving up the occupational ladder in the mills and outside of them, no matter what sort of work the individual wanted to do. It represented the difference between themselves and the people they came in contact with—foremen, shopkeepers, office workers, skilled tradesmen, doctors, lawyers, etc.—who held what seemed to them to be the better-paying and "easier" jobs in society.

As they viewed their jobs in steel as not being of their own choosing, they also viewed them as heavy, hard work. This was stressed again and again in the interviews [retired, age 74]:

Q. Of all the jobs you've had in steel plants, Mr. M., which one did you like best?

A. Well, if I had it to do over again, I'd never go into the sheet mills. That work is too hard and too hot. I was lucky because I never got cramps in my stomach, but sometimes I'd come home and couldn't raise my arms to reach my neck. My muscles would cramp up as big as my feet. That was hard work in those days—you'd move the steel by hand onto the rolls and pull it back and forth, hot steel, too.

Wife: He'd come home with his whole face burned sometimes.

Mr. M.: Many's the time I've come home feeling so bad I didn't think I would make it back. But my wife would work over me, and somehow I'd go back the next day. It never used to be so hard when I started there. We'd only do seven heats a day—105 pairs. Then they went up to seven, eight, nine, ten heats a day. When I quit, they were doing 400 pairs a day, and it was all by hand.

Q. Didn't some machinery come in before you left the sheet mill?

A. Only two things, a steam hammer to pound the doubles down and steam to cool the rolls. Before, when the rolls got too hot, we could take ten minutes off till they cooled down. With steam, though, they could be cooled down and still kept working. That was the trouble with the job. People tried to do as much as they could to earn more money. That made it such hard work. In Muncie the union had a limit of 11 heats a shift. One night one man did 12 heats, and the next night 13.

The other men got mad and pushed it up to 18 heats. That's too hard on a man.

Q. Was there anything you liked about the job?

A. No. I can't think of anything. It was hard, hot work, and I wouldn't go through it again.

Wife: Come now, honey, you couldn't have worked there all those years and not found something you liked?

Mr. M.: There is nothing I can think of—only the money. I couldn't think of anything else I could go into where I could earn as much money—it was good pay. Once I got started, I couldn't quit or I'd have had to start over some place else at the bottom.

Some of these men, as in the illustration above, stuck it out as long as they could, trying to hold on to the job which gave them the most pay. Others, as in the following case, were unable to stand the gaff and sacrified pay for an easier job [retired, age 65]:

Q. What was your job at Caltown Steel, Mr. K.?

A. I had lots of jobs; I worked all over the place, worked there thirty-nine years. I worked in the machine shop, sheet mill, foundry as janitor. I had lots of jobs, but I am glad to be quit now. I wouldn't go back.

Q. Why wouldn't you want to go back?

A. I worked hard. My arms and legs, they are all no good now. They hurt me when the weather changes. I was a shearer in the sheet mill for nine years, and all my muscles would cramp up. I ruined my arms there, went to the hospital a couple of times. I quit that job then and went to the foundry as molder and helper.

Q. Which of your jobs did you like best?

A. When I was young, I worked hard and liked to make money. I worked a couple of years in Plant No. 1, and they gave me a job as handyman in the machine shop at a little more money. Then I went to the sheet mill and was raised a little more. Each time, I got a little more money. But that job as shearer was too much. Here is what I did. (Mr. K. demonstrates working with the hot metal, cutting sheets with heavy pliers.) At the end of the day, when I had to make out my report, I tried to hold the pencil and write, and I couldn't do it. I had to ask someone else to make out the report for me. When I'd get home, I'd walk in the kitchen and just fall on the floor. After that, I did not care so much for money. On my jobs in the foundry I did not get so much money, but it was easy work. (Daughter enters room.)

Daughter: Dad used to do that a lot of times. (Referring to his falling on the floor when he got home from work.) It was just too hard for him. I work out there now, as a checker in the 14-inch mill. But things are a lot different now than they were. They did not have all the machines to do the work. The mill was just a load full of foreigners, and they all had to work hard.

Q. Which of your jobs did you like best, Mr. K.?

A. I liked being a janitor best. I did that for six years, just before I retired. That was easy work, even if it did not pay so much.

THE MEANING OF WORK

The one meaning of work apparent in the case of every man interviewed, then, was that of earning a living. From their point of view it was *the* reason why they were working in the

TABLE 5

MEANINGS OF WORK FOR STEELWORKERS

MEANINGS OF WORK*	EMPLOYED		RETIRED	TOTAL	PERCENT-AGE OF GROUP
	55–64	65 and Over			
1. Earning a living and none other..	22	5	17	44	34
2. Keeping busy..................	15	9	19	43	34
3, *a* and *b*. Self-respect and the re-spect of others................	10	4	10	24	19
4. Association..................	8	4	11	23	18
5, *a*. Sense of responsibility and im-portance......................	7	3	3	13	10
b. Satisfaction of a job well done..	2	2	3	7	5
c. New experience...............			1	1	1

* The meanings here listed were derived directly from the workers' own statements and therefore do not correspond exactly with the terminology of the meaning categories in Table 1 of chap. i. The numbers which precede the meanings indicate the equivalent meanings in Table 1.

mills. To attempt to rate it as more or less important than other meanings would be unrealistic. For some, as in the two cases cited above, it was the only meaning which their job had for them—the only part it played in their lives. These men stated their likes and dislikes in terms of the pay the job offered and the physical hardships involved in doing the job. Thirty-four per cent of the group indicated no meaning of work other than that of earning a living. But, for many, their work had come to have other meanings as well (Table 5).

Probably the most important meaning of work for this group

was that of keeping busy. For some this meant following a pre-scribed routine [hooker, age 58]:

Q. What will you miss about your job?

A. I'll miss my friends out there; and, mostly, I'll miss just not work-ing. Every time I look at the clock I'll think: I should be just starting work, or finishing, or doing this, or that; even on vacation now and on my days off I get tired just sitting around. One day is all right, but no more. I get to where I just wait for the time to go back to work. I keep looking at the clock, thinking what I should be doing at work.

For others "keeping busy" was bound up with the idea of working hard—almost a sense of physical well-being in working. A few of the men stated this emphatically; but in the following example the subject tried to account for it in other ways [hooker, age 56]:

Q. Which job did you like best, Mr. J., your job as ladleman or your job as a hooker?

A. I made more money as ladleman, but I like my job as hooker better. It's easier work for a man my age. I don't have to work very hard.

Q. Do you prefer easy work?

A. Sure! Why kill yourself working?

Wife: My husband likes to work. All the time he wants to do some-thing. Even on his days off he works; he does work around the house, or he'll go over and help his friends. Like tonight, he is going over to Hammond to help some friends paint their house.

Mr. J.: Oh, sure. A man has to do some work. I heard a doctor say on the radio the other day that, when a man stops working, he just wastes away and dies soon.

Q. What do you like most about working?

A. Well, you have to work if you want to earn money. If you have a family, you have to support them.

Q. Then why do you work on your days off?

A. (*Laughs.*) I would not know what to do with myself if I did not work. I still feel strong, not like when I was young, though. When I was young, I was as strong as a horse. I liked hard work then. Some-times, I even worked a double shift, to earn more money. I wouldn't be able to do it now, though. I like to lie down and rest a while when I feel like it.

Work meant association for many; it meant being with "the gang" [hooker, age 58]:

Q. Which of the jobs that you have had did you like best?
A. I just liked to work. I like being with men. There is no particular job I liked best, just being in steel. They are good men working in steel mills; no matter where you go, you find a good bunch of men.

For some holding a job was intimately bound up with their sense of self-respect. It maintained their position as head of the household; it determined their sense of worth. In the patriarchal system of family organization in Eastern Europe the man may have automatically been delegated the role of family head; however, in our society some of them found that it is really the wage-earner who is the head of the house [retired, age 71]:

Q. Would you have kept working at Caltown Steel if you could, Mr. B.?
A. Sure, I like to work; much better than staying at home. Some men are lazy. I can't sit around and do nothing. Who stays home! Women stay home, and children stay home. (*Imitates noise of children.*)It makes me mad. . . . It used to be different. I'd bring home $60 or $70 on a pay-day, and the kids would just jump with excitement. The old man had brought home a good pay.

(The daughter agreed with Mr. B. here; she explained that Mr. B. had seven daughters and one son and that he had had to work hard to keep his family going.)

Only a few men attached any sense of importance or responsibility to the job. Cases, as in the following example, where the men were able to relate their job to the operation of the total plant were rare [inspector, age 66]:

Q. What is your job at Caltown Steel?
A. I'm an oiler in the motor room.
Friend: That's an easy job. That's where he got his paunch.
Q. How long have you had that job?
A. I've been an oiler for eleven years steady. I've been at the plant twenty-one years.
Q. Do you like your job as oiler?
A. Oh, yes, I like to work around machines.
Q. Why?
A. That's hard to explain. I like to work with my hands, to feel that I can do something, something I know how to do. Our machines run the whole plant. If we shut down, the whole plant has to quit. It's an important job.

Most men had no feeling of accomplishment, no sense of having helped create a finished sheet of steel from the mounds of coal, ore, limestone, and scrap on the loading docks. One man summed it up as follows:

Q. Of all your different jobs, which did you like best?

A. I really think my job as tile-setter was the best I ever had. I got a real enjoyment out of that job because you were always doing something a little different and you had the satisfaction of seeing your work finished. One day you'd do a bathroom in coral. I never cared much for the color, but it made a beautiful room. The next day you'd do a room in blue, and, when you finished, you really had a beautiful room there too. The next day you'd do a room in peach, and that was beautiful too when you were finished. I liked starting the job and knowing that I'd finished it. In a steel plant you're never through. You finish one stack of sheets, and you turn around and there's another stack waiting. It's always the same job, too. You can't follow one thing through to the end. I'm not complaining, you understand, but I think I liked my job as a tile-setter best of all.

Most of these men related themselves to the job on hand and indicated no sense of identification with the steel industry as a whole. They might regard themselves as hookers, scarfers, crane men, shearers, etc.—but they were men who worked at a particular kind of job rather than men who produced steel. They had no symbols of their calling, no mythology, no folk heroes. Joe Magarac was just another Czech name to them— not the Paul Bunyan of steel.

Only a few native-born workers who had grown up in steel referred to the "mills" rather than to their job or their department. And these few claimed that the mills have changed [retired, age 67]:

Q. What was your old job?

A. I used to be a heater.

Q. What does a heater do?

A. I used to heat the ingots for the roller. It used to be one of the top jobs in the mill.

Q. Did you like it?

A. Oh, sure. It was a good job then. I used to make as much as $40 in one day back in 1918.

Q. Isn't it a good job any more?

A. It's not the same. The mills have changed. Two rollers do the work now that twenty used to do. It used to be a hand operation; now they have machinery that can roll a strip two blocks long. They can produce much more steel per roller today. But the type of man has changed. Why, I remember, back in 1911, they brought a roller in from Pittsburgh to do a job. This fellow was known from coast to coast. He not only was one of the finest rollers in the country; he also was a first-class heater, rougher, and cutter. He knew his steel and could do anything that could be done to a slab of hot steel. (Tells a story about the trouble the cutter was having with the steel this man was rolling. The cutter claimed that he was rolling at the wrong temperature and that the sheet wouldn't lie flat. So he rolled another ingot and cut it himself. "It came out flat, and as pretty as you please.") In those days, you had to know how to work the steel. Today all one has to know is how to operate the machine. They certainly are a lot more efficient now, but it's not the same as it used to be.

THE OLDER STEELWORKER AND RETIREMENT

Retirement benefits and practices have varied widely in the last ten years in this company, probably reflecting the changing attitude toward the older worker in industry as a whole during this period. Prior to World War II there was no explicitly stated retirement policy for hourly rated mill workers. Workers remained at their job without reference to chronological age for as long as they desired or until they were no longer able to perform their jobs satisfactorily. The decision to retire a worker was an individual one reached by the worker himself and his particular foreman or supervisor. However, it is likely that, in keeping with industrial practice at that time, the workers may have been encouraged to retire during times of labor surplus and to remain at their jobs in times of labor shortage. During the labor shortage of World War II, for example, men were allowed and, in many cases, encouraged to continue at their jobs beyond the age of 65. In April, 1946, however, the company first instituted a policy of compulsory retirement. The wartime group of workers over 65 were retired, and other workers were retired as they reached age 65.

Although the company has maintained some form of voluntary contributory retirement annuity plan since 1936,[7] there was no universal pension plan supplementary to Social Security until

7. However, until 1943, participation in the plan was limited to those workers with annual earnings of $3,000 per year or better. Thus, most of the workers at the unskilled and semiskilled job levels were not eligible. The voluntary contributory pension plan still continues, and the worker may choose between it and the noncontributory pension.

the last half of 1949. In 1949 the "pension" strike of the International Steelworkers' Union resulted in the adoption of the noncontributory pension plan which was agreed upon by all the major steel companies. The plan in effect at this mill provides that the company pay the difference between Social Security benefits and a minimum pension of $60 per month for workers with fifteen years' continuous service or more, and the difference between Social Security and a minimum of $100 for those with twenty-five years' continuous service or more. The contract negotiated by the union local with the company at this time also substituted a voluntary retirement plan for the age 65 compulsory retirement policy which was then in effect. The voluntary retirement plan provided that the worker be given his choice of retiring at age 65 or of continuing as long as he is able to perform his regular job.

The idea of retirement, then, is a relatively new one to the worker at this plant, and the various changes in retirement practices and benefits during the last ten years seem to have left the worker without any clear-cut notion of what to expect when he reaches retirement age. Some retirement counseling is done by the company personnel office in the form of pre-retirement interview. About six months prior to their sixty-fifth birthday, workers are called in for an interview with the personnel counselor. The purpose of this interview is to advise the employee as to the types and amounts of benefits available to him upon retirement and to obtain his decision as to whether he wants to continue working or retire. Some informal discussion of individual retirement plans and the problems may also be included in this interview. The union maintains a full-time pension grievance steward at their office who handles complaints about pension, insurance, and employment eligibility for its older members. Many of the men interviewed in this study looked to the union office for advice and information concerning retirement as well as for handling of grievances.

Despite these attempts of both the company and the union to prepare their older workers for retirement and to inform them of their rights and privileges upon reaching age 65, the results of the lack of any systematic or effective program of preparation and information are striking. For example, over 90 per cent of the group interview believed that they were only allowed to continue working for a maximum of three years past the age of 65. Many of the workers who retired prior to the signing of the present contract believed that the Social Security law at that time required all workers to retire at age 65; and some of the employed men under the age of 65 interviewed think that, if they continue working past 65, they will forfeit their rights to Social Security benefits or that the amount of Social Security payments due them will be reduced.

TABLE 6

ATTITUDE TOWARD RETIREMENT AT
AGE 65: EMPLOYED MEN

Attitude toward Retirement	No.	Per Cent
Want to retire..........	34	57
Don't want to retire....	19	32
Undecided.............	7	12
Total..............	60	....

For the purpose of our study, the lack of a long-standing, or even commonly understood, retirement policy in this plant would lead us to expect much confusion in the retirement attitudes and expectations of this group, and it may be likely that the uncertainties and ambiguities of these retirement practices and their indicated incomplete realization of the problems faced by the older worker could be typical of the situation prevailing in industry today.

ATTITUDES TOWARD RETIREMENT

The Employed Men under 65

When asked if they intended to retire when they reached 65, 57 per cent of the group indicated that they did, 32 per cent stated that they wanted to keep working, and 12 per cent were undecided (Table 6). Practically all the group who wanted to retire viewed retirement as a welcome relief from a lifetime of hard work. They reasoned that, after spending a good part of their lives in a steel mill, they were entitled to a rest before they died [crane operator, age 63]:

Q. Do you think you will retire when you reach 65?

A. Yes, I will. God bless the day I can leave the mill—I sure do want to retire.

Q. Why?

A. I want to move to Los Angeles and get away from this climate. It's too dirty to live here. It's not good for your health. My daughter lives in California now, in Los Angeles. My wife is visiting there now. That's a good place to live. I'll be glad to move.

Q. What do you think is the best age for a man to retire?

A. Sixty is best, so you can have a few years to enjoy life. Working every day in the mills is no good for you. You should have a few years before you die to enjoy yourself. You have to keep busy, though—not get stiff like some retired men I know. I will always work a couple hours a day, or walk a few blocks to get exercise. You don't live long if you get stiff from sitting around.

Q. What will you miss about your job when you leave?

A. Nothing. I'm tired of working every day all my life. I'm like a horse—I listen for bells and alarm clocks and jump whenever someone tells me to. That's no way to live. You don't do anything on your own, only what someone else tells you to do. I don't like that. I want to do something when I feel like it. I won't loaf, of course, even when I'm retired. I'll keep busy a little, doing something every day so I won't get stiff.

However, unlike the case cited above, about thirty of the thirty-four in this group had no well-worked-out plans for their retirement. Ten of them described their postretirement activities with such vague statements as, "I'll rest," or "I'll take it easy," or "I'll walk around and see my friends." The other twenty had some notion of what they would like to do or expected to do; these varied from statements such as, "I'll work around the house and garden," to thoughts of buying farms or moving to a better climate. Mostly, though, these were statements of intention rather than worked-out plans for execution. The idea of retirement was still new to most of them; it as yet had only the negative meaning of release from work. It was a source of concern to them, however—money, health, and keeping busy were their chief worries. Only six of this group felt that they were well prepared for retirement.

But beyond the desire to leave their jobs and a general unrest about the problems they would face after retirement, only a few of this group visualized retirement as a new way of life with satisfactions of its own.

Of the nineteen men who wanted to continue working past the age of 65, five replied that they would stay on only because they could not afford to retire. The other fourteen, however, stressed a different reason for wanting to remain at their jobs. Most of these men were of the conviction that a man had to keep on working if he wanted to live [stock marker, age 64]:

Q. Do you think you'll retire when you reach 65?
A. No, not if I can get a doctor to say I'm O.K. to go back to work. They have a plan now that you don't have to retire.
Q. At what age should men retire?
A. I don't think they should have to retire. Of course a lot of men died, but if a man is alive at seventy, he can still work.
Q. Why would you want to keep working?
A. Why? I'll tell you. Last year a man I know reached 65. Then they had to retire, even the big shots. But he told the foreman he wanted to go on working. The foreman told him: "Why the hell should you go on working? You have the house, the car, the family, the cash money—why don't you want to quit?" He answered: "Sure I have the money and the car, but I'm used to working. If I quit, I'll die in a little while." The foreman told him he had to quit anyway, and three months later he was dead. When a man's used to exercise and work, he can't just quit and do nothing. The only way to stay alive is to keep working.

Oddly enough, many men of both the group that wanted to retire at 65 and the group that wanted to continue working rationalized their choices in terms of "death." The first group stated that a man is entitled to some rest before he dies. However, they also felt that, if a man rested (i.e., stopped working), he would not have long to live. They, therefore, either qualified their desire to retire with the statement, "Of course I'll keep busy; a man has to keep busy," or else seemed resigned to the thought of dying and wanted to take their rest regardless of the consequences. The other group also stated that a man dies if he stops working, but they actually seemed afraid to stop working—afraid to stop the activity which they associated with life.

This preoccupation with death was particularly noticeable among those men who stressed "keeping busy" as a meaning of work. The ability to "keep busy" was one of their major concerns about retirement. Although income and health were also important in their thinking, their concerns with income or adequacy of pension and health (as it related to a specific ailment) were tangible ones; these were problems which they could identify, conjure with, and complain about. But the concern about "keeping busy" and, in some cases, the related concern about health (a generalized anxiety usually expressed as, "If my health is still O.K." or "If I live that long"—with the implication, "If I am able to keep busy") struck this writer as being a sort of "great uneasiness" troubling these men: an intangible fear against which they had no defense and could not even raise an effective objection. It seems that they equated "keeping busy" with "keeping alive" and feared that their failure to keep busy would result in death.

The Employed over 65

Of the men who have reached 65 since November, 1949—the date on which the noncompulsory retirement plan went into effect—about one out of seventeen have remained at their jobs past the "normal" retirement age. It does not follow that all the others wanted to retire at age 65. However, we do not know how many of these men were required to retire because they could not meet the company's physical requirements or retired because they did not clearly understand their right to continue on their jobs.

Of the eighteen men interviewed, seven indicated that the only reason they continued at their job was an inadequate income. Work was regarded as a burden by them and had little meaning other than earning a living; they would have retired at the earliest age at which they could have had an adequate pension [inspector, age 66]:

Mr. E.: What questions are you going to ask?

Interviewer: We're interested in finding out your opinions about retirement.

Mr. E.: A man can work as long as he feels good.

Q. Do you want to work as long as you feel good?

A. Well, I don't know how much longer I can work. I was sick for a year a couple of years ago. I was sick here (*points to his chest*). Anybody working out in the dust and the dirt of the mills is going to be troubled by it. I'm 66 now. I feel all right now, but if I don't feel good next year, I'll quit. Maybe I'll work a few more months.

Q. At what age do you think a man ought to retire?

A. At 55! A man should retire while he still has a few good years ahead of him. If a man works till 65, he doesn't have long to live—a year or two maybe. If a man can stop working and do the things that are healthful for him, he will live longer. A man will live longer if he doesn't work.

Q. Why did you keep working past 65?

A. How could I stop? No money. They tell me if I quit I get $93 pension. That's not enough to live on. I work in the mill since 1914, ever since I come to this country. Tomorrow I'll have been twenty-five years at Caltown Steel. But I don't have enough money to retire. Some of the fellows told me if I worked past 65, I'd have to work three years, otherwise they won't give me a pension. But I don't think they're right.

Q. How much pension do you think it takes for a man and wife to make out all right?

A. Well, you can't live on $100; not at these prices. A retired man doesn't spend as much money as a workingman. He doesn't need as much. When I work, I get tired. I have to drink. If I were retired, I wouldn't have to spend that. One hundred and fifty dollars would give you enough to live on. You wouldn't be able to do much, but you'd be able to live.

Son: Another fault with the pension system at Caltown Steel is that they stop the pension when the man dies. His widow doesn't get anything. The system they have on the police force, where work is much better, is that, if a man dies, they pay his widow his pension. The company certainly doesn't play fair with their retired men. . . .

Q. What do you think you'll miss about your job when you retire, Mr. E.?

A. What should I miss after thirty-seven years in the mill? I'll be sorry the pensions aren't any bigger—that's what I'll miss.

Q. What do you do now in your spare time and on Sundays?

A. Do? I don't do anything—I stay around the house and sit. Sometimes, I go driving with him. (*Indicates son, who is reading newspaper.*)

Q. What will you do after you retire? You'll have all day then.

A. I won't do anything; I'll be retired. I'll stay at home—go play a little cards with my friends and talk with them.

Q. Will you stay here in Lakeport?

A. Sure, where else could I go?

Q. Have you ever wanted to move to a small farm somewhere?

A. A farm? I've thought of moving to a farm, but my wife wants to stay here. She's lived here for forty years, and I've lived here for twenty-five. She doesn't want to move—it's her home.

Q. How much longer do you think you'll want to work?

A. Maybe a few more months—as long as I feel good. I still have trouble. My lungs went bad a couple of years ago, and lately I've had an ache across my shoulders. It's from the draft out there—you get sweaty, then go out to cool off right in the draft. I went to a doctor for six months for my back. He gave me medicines and shots and finally told me I'd been in a draft. I said: "I could have told you that six months ago. Why did you keep me coming back till I'd spent $300 and then tell me I've been in a draft?" These doctors are awful; it all depends on where they went to school. They all have something different to tell you. I asked one doctor what I should eat to keep healthy. He asked me if I drink. I said "yes." He said, "Well, I drink too—two or three quarts a month." I said, "Hell, I drink two or three quarts a week." So he says be sure to get good whiskey. But who can afford good whiskey?

Q. How long have you lived here in this house?

A. Sixteen years, here.

Q. Do you rent this apartment?

A. Yes.

(The interviewers prepared to leave. Mr. E. followed them to the door and spoke for several minutes on the desirability of having a retirement age of 50 years, so a man could travel and enjoy himself for a while before he died. "You boys will have to fight for it—I'm too old, now. A retirement age of 50 is best, and the company can afford it. I've made a lot of money for that company, and how much will they pay me? You boys, your work will pay my pension. The ones who come after you will pay your pension. There's no reason why you can't retire at 50 and get $200 a month pension if you fight for it.")

But retirement was an unknown quantity for these men. Although they knew they wanted to quit work, they had only the vaguest notion of what might come after. Perhaps some of them had put off retirement just because they were afraid of the unknown. On the whole they were unprepared for this new way of life; they had done little planning and were poorly informed and advised. One of the seven in the group did not even have an approximate idea of the amount of pension he was entitled to [sweeper, age 66]:

Q. Did you want to keep working after you were 65?

A. They sent me to the doctor. The doctor says I can work six more months. The company called me in for an interview. They tell me I better quit. I tell them the doctor says I can work another six months. I go to CIO. They tell me I can get $100 pension. But I don't know what to think. Someone else tells me I get $1.00 pension for each year I work. That's only $30. I can't live on $30. My boss tell me to stay on working. So I stay. Maybe the company wants to save the pension. They call me in to the doctor again a little while ago. But he don't say anything this time. I keep working. Maybe this time they push me out at the end of the six months. . . .

Q. How long do you think you'd want to go on working at your job?

A. Maybe I quit January 25, on my birthday.

Q. Why do you want to quit?

A. I work long time, I retire.

Q. Do you think you'll miss not working at Caltown Steel?

A. No, I've had enough. I don't like to stay around the house, but I quit anyhow.

Q. What will you do with your time after you retire?

A. I don't know. Maybe I do jobs. I paint houses, cut grass, wash windows. People know me here. They give me jobs to do.

Q. You'll want to stay in Caltown, then?

A. Sure, people know me here. I get jobs here. All my friends are here.

Q. How much a month do you think it will cost you to live after you retire?

A. I don't know. It's hard to live on $90 or $100 a month. Rents are high. But retired men don't spend much. They don't buy clothes or go to night clubs. I do jobs; I get the money I need.

For eleven of the group, however, income was not the only reason they remained at their jobs. Work for these men meant activity—activity which kept them alive [bolt-cutter, age 66]:

Q. Do you think you'll ever want to retire?

A. I like to work; I don't want to retire. I have to keep at my job and keep working.

Q. Do you like your job in the machine shop?

A. Sure, it's a good job. I don't care what job I have as long as I can work.

Q. Why do you want to go on working?

A. I've always worked. I've always had a job. I left home when I was 16 and got my first job. That was in 1899.

Q. Would you miss not working if you ever decided to retire?

A. Sure I'd miss not working. A man has to have something to do—you live longer if you're working.

Q. Do you think men ought to retire?

A. Not as long as they still can work. If a man can work, he ought to. Some men can't do any work after they're 50, so they should retire; but not a man who is still healthy.

Q. What would you do with yourself if you had to retire from Caltown Steel?

A. I'd look for another job.

Q. What job?

A. Any job—I don't care what job I do, as long as I can work.

The lives of these men had come to center about the activity of work. Without such activity retirement could hold little satisfaction for them.

TABLE 7

ATTITUDE TOWARD RETIREMENT AT
AGE 65: RETIRED MEN

Did He Retire prior to November, 1949?	Did He Want To Retire?		
	Yes	No	Total
Yes..........	5	32	37
No..........	7	6	13
Total.....	12	38	50

The Retired Men

Thirty-seven of the group of fifty retired men interviewed were retired during the 1946–49 interval when retirement was compulsory at age 65. When asked if they wanted to retire at that time, thirty-two of the thirty-seven stated that they did not, and five said that they did. Of the men who retired since November, 1949, seven indicated that they wanted to retire at 65, and six were forced to retire because they could not meet the company's physical requirements. Therefore, only twelve of the fifty men interviewed either chose to retire or indicated that they were willing to retire at the time that company policy required them to (Table 7).

As might be expected, those men who regarded work only as a way of earning a living and who had at least a barely adequate retirement income were well satisfied with retirement. But retirement was not only an escape welcomed by those men for whom work was nothing more than the earning of a living. At least six of the retired group found satisfactions in retirement which adequately replaced the association, activity, and new experience which their jobs held for them [retired, age 66]:

Q. Have there been things you have missed about your job since you've been retired?

A. No, I've liked being retired too much.

Q. Would you have wanted to stay on after 65 if you could have had your old job as assistant roller?

A. No. (*Laughs.*) I was offered plenty of good jobs, but I wanted to retire. A man shouldn't work after 65; he should take it easy and enjoy what little time he has left. Why, I know an old Irishman, a retired cop. He is 70 now and is working as a plant guard. They say he has $50,000 in the bank. I saw him the other day and said, "Hey, Mike, I hear you are still working, how come?" He said, "Oh, a man has to earn some money!" I said, "What for?" He said, "Oh, you always need money." I said, "Why, Mike, don't you know that you can't take it with you? When you die, they give you a suit that has no pockets in it, so you can't keep it there. And they fold your hands across your chest where they can see them, and they know you have no money there either. It won't do you any good." But there is no reasoning about that. He is just one of these crazy fellows who wants to keep on working.

Q. When do you think a man ought to retire?

A. I think 60 is a good age. That gives the man a little time. When it came time for me to retire, the fellows at the plant said, "What makes you think you are going to retire? Why, you won't know what to do if you aren't working." I told them I knew just what I was going to do. I was going to buy a rocking chair and set in it in the living room. Then I'd get a comfortable pair of slippers and sit down and rock all day.

Q. Where is it?

A. What?

Q. Your rocking chair?

A. Oh (*laughs*), I never got it. I found too many other things to do.

Q. What do you do with yourself now?

A. Oh, pretty much what I want to do. I just returned from a two-week fishing trip up in northern Michigan. I like to fish, and I like to watch ball games and sports events of all kinds. Sometimes, when I am out in the streetcar, I pass a sandlot ball game; then I get off and spend a few hours watching. I like to go out to the big-league games, too. I thought maybe I'd go along and watch the White Sox on their next road trip. I'd go from city to city with them and see their games.

Q. Do you find that your pension is enough to let you do the things that you want to do?

A. Yes, a single man can get along all right on $100 a month. But, besides that, I have bonds and savings. I have enough to live on and do the things I want to. I don't have to account to anybody. I come and go as I please.

Q. Are you single then?

A. Yes, I live here with my sister and brother-in-law. He is the one who works at Metropolis. This is an eight-room apartment, so there is room for me.

But also included in the group of twelve who wanted to retire were at least two men who found no satisfaction in retirement. Crippled and alone, living on a pension that was barely sufficient to keep them alive, and without any provision for medical care, these men could find no satisfaction in either work or retirement. The following case is a dramatic illustration. It is exceptional only because of the severity of the factors confronting this man. But the same factors—poverty, ill-health, loss of meaningful activity, and loneliness—were threats for most of the retired men interviewed. They had, thus far, escaped the full effects of all four; but, for many, the escape may be only a temporary one [retired, age 78]:

(Mr. B. lives in a shanty of two rooms attached to the side of a large two-story frame apartment house located on a rather run-down street close to the business section. The rooms of Mr. B.'s shanty are dirty, the furniture ancient and moth-eaten. There are no toilet facilities, and only an old wood stove to supply heat. The kitchen, in the rear room, had an electric light, but the interviewer observed none in the front room. Mr. B. himself is an old, senile-looking man, short and pudgy, with a white stubble of beard and sparse gray hair. His blue work clothes were dirty and ragged, and his shoes were cut down the front and sides to allow for his swollen, arthritic feet and ankles. Mr. B. answered the interviewer's knock slowly, shuffling his feet along the floor and tapping his cane unsteadily in front of him. He spoke throughout the interview in thick but quite intelligible English and referred to the interviewer continually as "young fellow." He seemed not to comprehend the nature of the interview or its purpose, even after the introduction was repeated.)

Q. How long have you been retired from Caltown Steel?

A. Five years or so; I can't remember. (His first reply to most questions was, "I don't know" or "I can't remember." If given time, however, he usually supplied an answer.)

Q. Did you want to retire?

A. What do you mean, did I want to retire? I came to work one day, when I was 65, and the boss says: "George, you have to quit work after today and take your pension." They made everybody 65 quit at the same time. Sixteen men, all at the same time.

Q. Would you have kept on working if you could have?

A. Maybe a little longer. But I didn't mind quitting. I worked hard.

Q. Does your pension give you enough to live on?

A. I'll tell you the honest truth, young fellow. I get $95 a month. Forty-one dollars and ten cents from the company and $53.90 from the United States. (Mr. B. quoted these figures with emphasis, as though to underline their inadequacy.) I can't live on that. I buy a few clothes (*plucks at worn shirt*), pay my rent; so, lots of times, I just won't have any money. Things cost too much now. I can't live on $95 only. But that's all I get. I used to get $80 or $85 a month, and I raised a family. But now, things are too high.

Q. What do you think is a fair pension?

A. Twenty dollars more a month would be good. That would be enough for me.

Q. If you could have got that much money when you were 65, would you have wanted to retire?

A. What do you mean, money to retire? The boss tells me, "George, after tonight you stay at home and take your pension."

Q. Have you ever tried to get another job?

A. No, I never tried. My legs are too bad. I can't work any more.

Q. What do you do during the day now?

A. I get up, cook a little, go out and carry coal and break up wood for kindling. Then I sit in my shanty. I don't bother to keep it clean. (Here Mr. B. waved his arm toward the dirty walls, the unswept floors, and the untidy kitchen.) I used to live in the big house (*points to indicate house to which shanty is joined*) with my wife; but when my wife died, seventeen years ago, I moved in here. The landlord told me I could have this shanty. But I have to pay $18 or $16, I forget which, for the two little rooms.

Q. Do you ever see any of your old friends?

A. No. They're all dead. My one son lives somewhere on Broadway (street in Caltown). Sometimes he visits me. My daughter lives in Metropolis. Sometimes, she visits me. But I'm just the old man to them. Last February I almost died, I was so sick. My son came to visit then. It was a cold day. I had to go out to pay my gas bill. I had only this old coat. (He pulled a shabby work jacket from the floor and showed it to the interviewer.) I walked out on the sidewalks; I could hardly move, it was so slippery. I got up to the bank, but I could not go any further. I froze my finger while carrying my cane. (Mr. B. pointed to a blue fingernail on his right hand to indicate the frozen finger.)

(When the interview drew to a close and the interviewer got up to leave, Mr. B. looked around almost desperately, saying, "Please, help me. I cannot live on $95 a month.")

However, thirty-eight, or 75 per cent, of the fifty retired men stated that they did not want to quit their jobs at the time they were forced to retire. Twenty-three of them had tried to find other jobs after they left the mills, and eleven were employed at the time of the interview. But they found that few places were willing to hire older men. Oddly enough, the few places in the vicinity which employed older workers actually were eager to obtain them, and some even went so far as to solicit their services at the time of their retirement from the steel plant. First of these was the local city government, for whom four of these men were working or had worked. They were employed on a part-time basis doing road work or street-cleaning. These jobs were of an uncertain duration and apparently "political" appointments. The other willing employer of older workers mentioned was a local car-loading company which, according to some of the men interviewed, preferred older workers, since they were willing to work "harder" than the younger men and did jobs that the younger men were unwilling to do. None of the men interviewed, however, liked the jobs they held with either of these employers.

Of the thirty-eight men who wanted to continue work at the time of their retirement, twelve said that they wanted to remain at their jobs only because they could not afford to retire [retired, age 74]:

Q. How long have you been retired from Caltown Steel?

A. Oh, I guess about five years now. They retired me on April 1, 1946. They laid off a whole group of men who were over 65 at that time. They had let these men keep on working during the war because there was a shortage.

Q. Why did you retire?

A. (*Shrugs shoulders.*) Why did I retire? I didn't retire; they retired me. (*Laughs.*) They laid off a whole bunch of us, all over 65. I was 68 then. They would not let me stay on.

Q. Did you want to retire?

A. No, I didn't want to retire. But they did not ask me; they laid me off.

Q. Why did you want to keep on working?

A. If you work, you get paid. You can't live on the pension they give you. Why else would I want to go to work for the city?

Q. What do you do for the city?

A. I work; I clean streets. It's hard work for an old man, but that's what they give me to do.

Wife: Do you want to give my husband a job? Do you want to give him a bigger pension?

(Interviewer explains purpose of interview to Mrs. M.)

Q. How long have you been working for the city, Mr. M.?

A. Since I left Caltown Steel. I don't know how long I'll stay with them, though. There is an election this month, and if a new mayor gets elected, we'll probably lose our jobs. He'll put his own friends in.

Q. Would you have gone to work for the city if you'd had enough pension to get along on when you retired?

A. Who can live on what I get? What do they give me? My pension was just raised to $93. How can you live on that? I burned twelve tons of coal this winter. The price of food is higher than it has ever been. I have taxes, gas, and electric bills to pay.

Wife: How can we afford to buy new clothes? Our clothes are worn out, but there is not enough money left to buy new ones.

Q. How much do you figure that you need to get along on comfortably, Mr. M.?

A. I don't know. I can't get along on what I get now; I need a little more. That's why I am working now.

Q. Would you have rather worked for Caltown Steel if they had let you?

A. Sure. But I am 74 now. There is nothing I could do for them.

Q. How long did you work there?

A. Oh, I worked there for a long time. I was there for about twenty-three years.

Q. Where did you work before that?

A. I worked at the Lakeport Steel Foundry. I had the same job that I always had at Caltown Steel. I worked in steel mills ever since I came to this country forty-five years ago from Lithuania.

Q. Did you come right to Caltown?

A. No, I went to Metropolis first. I worked in the steel mill there. I was a laborer. It was not much different though from the work I did at the Lakeport Steel Foundry and at Caltown Steel.

Q. Why did you want to go to work in a steel mill?

A. Why? You don't ask why. If you want to eat, you have to work. If you want to work, you take the job you can get.

Q. Do you ever miss not being back at Caltown Steel?

A. No. I don't miss my job there. I'd much rather work there though than clean streets. That's not the right kind of a job for an old man.

Q. When do you think a man ought to retire?

A. I can't afford to retire.

Q. If you had had a large enough pension to live on when you were 65, would you have retired?

A. Sure, why work? You work to get money. If you have enough money, you don't have to work.

Q. Are there any things you would like to do now if you did not have to work?

A. No, nothing in particular. I just take it easy and rest. I am tired; I am an old man now.

Q. What do you do in your spare time now?

A. I don't do much. I take it easy; I do a lot of work around the house though. It keeps me pretty busy.

(The interview drew to a close as Mr. M. prepared to go to work. He said in conclusion: "You are interested in finding out if men want to keep on working. If I had enough to live on, I would have retired a long time ago. But if I had to work, I would have wanted to stay at Caltown Steel. I still had a few good years left in me when they made me retire. It would have been better work than cleaning streets for an old man.")

For at least twenty-six of the thirty-eight men, however, income was not the only factor important in their desire to continue working past retirement age. Undoubtedly, some of them had at one time looked forward to retirement. But some, as in the following case, soon found life to be empty without the activity of work [retired, age 71]:

Q. Why did you retire?

A. I was 65 years old; they made me retire. They made everybody retire when they were 65.

Q. Would you have kept on working if they had let you?

A. Yes, I asked them to let me; but they would not. I went over to the CIO office and told them about it. But they couldn't do anything for me either.

Q. Why did you want to keep on working?

A. I did not have enough money. My company pension is $22, and, with Social Security, I get $84 a month. That is not enough to live on.

Q. How much pension do you think a man should have?

A. I can't live on $84 a month. I own this house; I rent the apartment upstairs and downstairs. But that just gives me enough to pay the mortgage. (Wife called in from the other room that the rental is just enough to pay the mortgage.) We pay all our bills, and then we have hardly enough left over for food. I have one pair of shoes; I need new shoes. (*Points to the heavy, well-worn work shoes that he was wearing at the time.*)

Q. What do you think a fair pension would be?

A. One hundred and forty-five dollars should be enough.

Q. If you could have had enough to live on, when you were 65, would you have wanted to retire?

A. Who can afford to retire at 65? A single man, maybe, who drinks all the time. You see them out in the park there, drunk all the time.

Q. Well, if you had had enough to live on, would you have retired?

A. Sure I'd retire. (*Laughs.*)

Q. Did you do any work after you were 65?

A. Yes, I worked three years at the Lakeport Carloading Company. I did labor there. I lifted heavy loads, cleaned washrooms, did anything they wanted me to do.

Q. Why did you leave?

A. I had an accident. A door fell on me. (*He traces a line across his head.*) It was too heavy work for an old man.

Q. Would you take another job if you could get one?

A. Sure; I go over to the CIO office many times. But they don't do anything for me. I am an old man; I can only do light work.

Q. Would you take a job as a sweeper?

A. Sure, but I can't get a job. I'd like to work at Caltown Steel. I've been over there several times. It's a good place to work for, but they don't have a job for me.

Q. How long have you lived in this house?

Son: Five years. We used to live down by the plant for twenty years before that. When my dad retired, he sold that house and moved here.

Q. Have you ever thought of moving from Caltown?

Son: He says the only time he will ever move from here is to go to (neighboring town). That's where the funeral parlor is, hey, Dad? He should not talk that way.

Mr. P.: I'm 71 years old; I only have a few more years.

Q. Do your friends live around here?

Son: Only his family. He does not see anyone else. He goes out and watches the card games in the park during the summer. He stands out on the sidewalk, just standing around. He spends most of his time with the chickens. He has chickens, doves, and pigeons in the back yard. If it weren't for these chickens, he wouldn't have anything to do. For the first three months after he retired, he spent all his time just walking up and down in the living room. He could not stand it having nothing to do. (Wife calls in to the interviewers from the other room: "You wait until you retire, see if you have anything to do!")

Q. (*To son.*) What does he miss most about his job—the income or something to do?

Son: Oh, something to do. He can't sit around the house; he'd rather work. Just two weeks ago he went to a tavern that a friend of mine owns, and he asked for a job sweeping and cleaning up. He would have gotten it but for one thing. The fellow said there was a lot of lifting of barrels to do, and he cannot do that heavy work anymore.

Mr. P.: I felt all right after I quit Caltown Steel. Then I worked in a car company and got hurt. I spent six weeks in the hospital. They like old fellows at the car company. They do anything they ask them to do—clean the washroom or anything—and they don't talk back. They make them lift heavy loads and do hard work. These young fellows won't do it—they quit. All my strength seemed to leave me after I got hurt, though. I have not felt strong since then.

Son: But he is willing to do light work, anything he can handle. Those chickens take all his time. (*To father.*) Dad, when the men go down, show them your chickens. (*To interviewers.*) He has got a whole flock of chickens and ducks. (*Imitates sound of ducks.*) They sure make noise, and the chickens do, too. If they took these chickens away, he'd die the next day.

For the married men of this group retirement meant staying in the house, staying where the "woman is"—it was a denial of their basic role of the male. In a town which made no provisions for its older citizens, there was no escape from the house for them except to "walk the streets" or, as in the above example, to find a refuge in a back-yard chicken coop or in "working" around the house and garden. Even the simple pleasures of the movies and the tavern were almost prohibitively expensive for many of them; and such luxuries as fishing, hunting, ball games, and travel were out of the question. Their pensions kept them alive at a meager subsistence level, giving them absolutely no protection against the financial burdens of illness and hospitalization. Nor did their wives contribute much to their sense of personal security, since the wives were faced with the discontinuance of their husband's pension upon their death. This would leave them only with an income of about $25 per month from the federal Social Security program.

The single men of this group fared no better than the family men. They lacked even the house and garden to consume their time. Having no family group to turn to, they were dependent on the community to fill their recreational, housing, and employment needs. But the community was built around the mills rather than the men who ran them. The residential sections were in between the mills and foundries of the town, located, without regard to living values, in the areas that industry did not want. The outer sections of the interstices were occupied by the homes of family men; the single men lived in the cheap hotels, boarding houses, and sleeping rooms in the center of the town nearest to the mills.

And, in a sense, their nonwork lives were also interstitial to the operation of the mills. The places that they slept, ate, and amused themselves were just temporary resting places between their periods of work at the mill. When they were retired by one mill, they tried to find a job at another. When they were refused work because of their age, there was little left for them in the life of the town crowded between the mills. Perhaps they wandered the streets, aimlessly looking for a friendly face or often just walking for the sake of activity—without direction, purpose, or hope. One respondent summed it up by saying: "In good weather you see them out there walking the streets, walking from one end of town to the other, walking themselves to death." Sometimes, they stopped to rest in one of the small barren "parks" which were located between mills. There they played cards, talked with other men who were also wanderers, or else just sat alone—staring at the ground. There were few other places in this industrial town which offered a retired man activity, recreation, companionship, or even rest.

The Greeks were most fortunate in having several restaurants in town which served as coffee-houses in the European tradition. The other men were dependent on the taverns of towns and an occasional bartender who felt kindly toward "the old guys who used to work at the mills," sometimes even setting them up drinks when they were short of cash. About the only other place in which they felt welcome was a bookmaking establishment in the slums of town. The owner, in this case, was particularly sympathetic to the plight of the retired man. (He probably had more insight and better understanding of their situation than any other person in town to whom this observer talked.) He would allow them to spend a good part of the day in his place, sitting, playing cards, watching television, talking with their friends. He knew them by name, and a warm, joking relationship existed between them. He would even lend them fairly large sums of money when they were faced with an economic crisis, such as hospitalization, for which they were totally unprepared and had no hope of assistance [retired, age 67]:

Mr. M.: What is it you want? I'll speak to you about anything you want. I don't hide anything.

(Proprietor had told Mr. M. about the interviewers after their first call at his combination liquor store and handbook. There seemed to be a warm relationship between the storeowner and Mr. M., the latter having borrowed money from the proprietor on one occasion to pay a hospital bill.)

Q. How long have you been retired?

A. I've been retired two years and a half.

Q. Did you want to retire?

A. No, I didn't want to retire, but I couldn't work. I hurt myself; I have a hernia, and the doctor won't let me work. I went to the company office and tried to get a job, but they wouldn't let me work.

Q. But would you have wanted to work if they'd let you?

A. Yes, I'd want to work, but I'd have to do a light job. Heavy work is no good for me. (Repeats story of hernia; also adds that he got the hernia while working on his job as a blacksmith's helper.)

Q. When do you think a man ought to retire?

A. (*Shakes head.*) I don't think a man ought to retire. I think a man ought to keep on working. You feel good when you work—you live longer.

Q. If you could have got a big pension, say, $200 a month, would you still have wanted to go on working?

A. It makes no difference how much pension I could get, I would still keep on working. You work, you keep busy—you feel good. I'd work today if not for my legs. You stop working and you die pretty quick. There's not much left for me now.

Q. What do you do with yourself now?

A. Nothing! I don't do nothing. Sometimes, I go over here. Sometimes, I go to the park. Then I looked after John's store for him a month ago. John is my good friend—I help him out. If a man treats me right, if he's an honest man, I stick with him. John (the owner of the shop) lent me $300 in 1942. I paid him back, but I always do what I can to help him.

Q. Do you make out all right on the pension you get?

A. I get $81 a month. Social Security gives me $59, and Caltown Steel only gives me $22. That's all they give me—that company is no good. I tell you, they make money on us.

Q. How much a month do you think would be a fair pension right now?

A. For a low-class man like me, $100 would be enough. I don't need much, and that would give me what I want.

Q. John says that you're going down to Hot Springs pretty soon?

A. Yes, I have a little money saved. I go down there—maybe I stay down there. For $25 a month down there, you can get a room with stove and refrigerator. I stay at the same place for twenty-seven years now, ever since it was built. I eat out—even for an old man it costs $2.25 or $2.50 a day to eat. How can I do that on what I make? If I find a job to help out, they stop my Social Security when I earn more than $50 a month. One of the taverns offered me a job of janitor, but I won't take it. I'm going to Hot Springs; I can live better on my pension. I can take baths down there, too, for my legs. In Lakeport baths are $2.00. In Hot Springs you can get thirteen for $20—that's about $1.20 a bath.

For most of the single men and many of the family men who stated that they did not want to retire, the activity of work had no substitute in retirement. Even though their job may have seemed a burden and without meaning during most of their lives, it was the activity of work that they missed in retirement. For it was work that organized and gave direction to their lives. They had no outside activities, interests, or satisfactions which would replace it.

III

The Meanings of Work and Retirement for Coal-Miners[1]

SOUTHERN Illinois has been a major coal-producing area for more than fifty years. At the present time nearly half of the thirty-one thousand Illinois coal-miners are employed in the area to the southeast of St. Louis, and more than 90 per cent of these work in four contiguous counties within a radius of less than forty miles.[2] This report describes a representative group of older men employed by the mining companies within these counties.

The mines of the area may be conveniently divided into those which are locally owned and produce on a small scale for local markets and those which are large-scale industrial enterprises controlled from distant metropolitan centers and which produce tens of millions of tons of coal annually for export to other parts of the country. The large mines each involve capital investments of from three to eight million dollars.[3] They have completely abandoned the ancient technology of pick and shovel; their methods today are those of the electric motor, the belt line, and the semiautomatic machine. Recent official reports indicate that pick miners are no longer employed in any of

1. Financial support for this study was provided by Southern Illinois University. The writer wishes to express his appreciation to the students who assisted in the collection of data and to the officials of the several mining companies and of the United Mine Workers of America for their advice and co-operation.

2. Department of Mines and Minerals, *Coal Report of Illinois for 1950* (Springfield, 1951). The four counties are Franklin, Perry, Saline, and Williamson.

3. Federal Reserve Bank of St. Louis, *Monthly Review*, August, 1949.

the mines with which this study is concerned. The work of the miner continues to be physically strenuous and hazardous, but it is technologically very different from that of fifty years ago.

More men are engaged in mining in southern Illinois than in any other occupation. There are no large cities within the area; the leading trade centers range from 5,000 to 15,000 in population. By census classification the population is almost equally distributed among rural, rural nonfarm, and urban settlements. This limited urbanization, in comparison with the nation as a whole, reflects the essentially nonurban character of the coal industry, which neither depends upon nor stimulates the growth of cities in the immediate vicinity. At the same time only a few of the smaller communities may today be described as "mining towns"; the economy of most of the villages and of all the larger towns is diversified by wholesale and retail establishments and increasingly by light manufacturing industries.[4]

These brief remarks must stand as a background for the report which follows. The demography and economic organization of the area are of only indirect interest here, although the reader may find significant indications of regional characteristics and institutional patterns.

DESCRIPTION OF THE STUDY

Scope and Method

The study was conducted during the first six months of 1951. Four of the largest mining companies, controlling twelve mines scattered over the four principal mining counties, were selected on the basis of the location, size, and type of their mining operations. Together they employed approximately 6,700 men; employment at individual mines ranged from 200 to 1,200 men. All the mines were of the "deep" or shaft type rather than the "strip" or surface type.[5]

4. Cf. Works Progress Administration, *Seven Standard Coal Towns* ("Research Monographs," No. 23 [Washington, 1941]).

5. Working conditions and job characteristics are so different in the two types of mines as to constitute separate industries in nearly every respect except the product.

With the approval of local union officials, company officers provided lists of men in their employ; these were compiled by selecting each tenth name of men over 50 years of age from current payroll records. From the combined list of 329 names so obtained, each second individual was designated to be interviewed. Interviews were held with the miner himself in his own home by university students who had had formal training in interview methods. The students added sixteen interviews to the selected list from their personal acquaintances or family members. A prepared schedule was completed in the course of the interview, and verbatim reports of the accompanying discussion were written as soon as possible thereafter.

The 186 men who were interviewed lived in ten major towns and some fifteen smaller villages. They represent approximately 3 per cent of all miners 50 years of age and over in southern Illinois. In terms of age distribution, proportion employed in underground and surface jobs, and total number of men employed as miners in various communities, the sample is believed to be representative of the older miners of the area. There are no recent occupational data by age groups which would permit an exact comparison with the study group[6]

General Characteristics of the Group

Table 8 shows certain major characteristics of the group; the following paragraphs present additional details related to these data.

The age range was from 50 to 76 years, with a median of 59 years. Nearly half of the group had reached or passed the age of 60, at which they became eligible for the miners' pension. Men aged 65 and over had come into the industry during the period of most rapid expansion from 1900 to 1910; men

6. By combining 1950 census data with industry reports, it is possible to estimate that the median age of all Illinois miners in 1950 was between 46 and 47 years. There were probably about 7,400 miners in southern Illinois over age 46; a one-tenth sample would total 740. The companies providing names employed slightly less than half of the area's miners; the sample of 329 appears close to the number which would be expected (*Sixteenth Census, 1940*, Vol. III, Part II, p. 905; *Bituminous Coal Annual, 1950* [Washington: Bituminous Coal Institute, 1950], p. 144).

in their fifties had entered during the first World War. The group includes only two men over 70 years of age.

Three-fourths of the group were native-born. The foreign-born came mainly from Italy, with a much smaller proportion from the British Isles. One-fifth of the native-born had migrated to Illinois from other states. Ninety-five per cent of the foreign-born had lived in the same communities for twenty-five years or more; all the native-born had lived in southern Illinois for more than twenty-five years.

TABLE 8

CHARACTERISTICS OF STUDY GROUP ACCORDING TO PERCENTAGE
IN VARIOUS SUBCATEGORIES

Classification Characteristics	Per Cent of Total Group
Age:	
Age group 50–59	53
Age group 60–76	47
Foreign-born 60 years of age and over	59
Native-born 60 years of age and over	29
Place of birth:	
Illinois	55
Other states, United States	21
European countries	24
Residence:	
Lived 25 years or longer (a) in southern Illinois	99
(b) in present community	88
Marital status and household constitution:	
Married and living with wife	93
Children born to men ever married (a) None or 1	27
(b) 2, 3, 4	57
(c) 5 or more	16
Households with 1 or more children under 21 years	31
Subjects with 2 or more dependents at time of study	31
Education:	
Left school before age 12	27
Continued in school after age 16	27
Completed less than three years of school	11
Completed more than twelve years of school	1
Work history and employment status:	
Occupation of subject's father (a) Miner	31
(b) Farmer	59
(c) Other	14
Began work as miner by age 18	58
Never employed in other occupation as much as one year	79
Job grade above median of current pay scale	24
Location of job at mine (a) underground	78
(b) on surface	22
Status at time of interview (a) regularly employed	91
(b) laid off, ill, just retired	9
Company by which employed: Company A, 5 mines	58
Company B, 4 mines	18
Company C, 1 mine	12
Company D, 2 mines	7
Other companies	4

The proportion of men married and with wife living is unusually high for this age level; there were only twelve widowed, divorced, or single men. Three-fifths of the households consisted of husband and wife only; but one-third of all households and one-fourth of those of men over 60 reported minor dependent children. One-tenth of the men had three or more dependents; less than 1 per cent had no dependents. Nearly 95 per cent of the men owned their homes.

Then men had left school at a median age of 14 years, having completed less than seven years of schooling; however, only 5 per cent had never attended school. In contrast, the children of these men had completed an average of eleven years of school, and 11 per cent had attended college.

Twenty-six per cent of the group, consisting mainly of the foreign-born, were Catholic. Half of the Protestants were Baptist, one-fourth Methodist, and one-seventh Disciples of Christ.

The mean age at which the men had first entered the mines was 19 years; the median was 17 years. Nearly all (98 per cent) had been employed as miners for twenty years or more. The average length of employment as a miner was 40 years. The great majority of men were the sons of farmers and miners; a few came from families of small businessmen and of laborers in other industries; none were sons of professional men, skilled craftsmen, or white-collar workers.

Official mining reports list more than sixty broad classifications of jobs in mechanized mines. The men of this group represent all of these as well as most of the subclasses.[7] For purposes of this study, men were ranked in terms of the pay scale for their jobs as established in current company-union contracts. Generally speaking, the underground production workers receive the highest pay rates, and the surface and maintenance workers the lowest.

The group includes only three Negroes, all of whom were employed at the same mine.

Although other numerical characteristics of the group will be presented from point to point throughout the report, the major

7. The group does not include officials, supervisors, or office employees; it does include gang bosses and face bosses and mine examiners employed by the companies. The term "foreman" is not commonly used in the industry.

portion of the discussion relates to descriptive materials obtained in interviews. The many statements quoted are taken directly from the interviewers' reports. It is important to emphasize that each of the quotations in paragraph form within each section is a comment made by a different individual; they are not consecutive parts of the same interview.

WORK EXPERIENCES

Becoming a Miner

The group represented mainly two general types of backgrounds. The first was the family in which the father and perhaps brothers were miners; 31 per cent of the men were sons of miners. The son usually was taken into the mine to work alongside his father, not as a wage-earner in his own right, but to add to the daily output of coal credited to his father. It was a matter of pride to a boy eventually to be given "his own number."

Men who were sons of miners spoke as follows:

Dad took me to work with him. At that time they were paid by the ton of coal. By taking me as his buddy, he was able to load more cars. I didn't do too much work at first, only helped by picking up coal with my hands and throwing it into the cars. Dad did most of the work.

I went to work in the mines when I was 16 years old. That was in 1911. We did solid shooting. The old man would have to tamp the ground for me and gauge the powder. We worked in water halfway up to our knees, for 32 cents a ton, and walked five miles there and five miles back every day. Kind of a hard way to make a living.

There's an old woman up the street who says she can still remember me starting for the mine with my dad with my lunch bucket dragging along on top of the snow.

The second type of background, from which came the largest proportion of the men, was the small subsistence farm in the vicinity of the mines. The opening of mines in the area after 1900 created job opportunities which no other industries offered. Boys from nearby farms and villages were drawn to the mines by the prospect of good wages.[8] Nearly 55 per cent of this group were the sons of farmers.

8. The early period of development of mining in the area was one of collective excitement in several respects—land speculation, business expansion, and

There wasn't anything but mining and farming here when I grew up, and mining paid the best.

I entered the mines because there was a big boom of mining then, and that was about the only job there was to do.

I started mining at 16, and I've worked at it for forty-three years now. That's about the only kind of life I've ever known about. In fact, that's about the only thing a young man in my day and time could do around here. It was either go to work in the mines or leave the country altogether to find work someplace else.

A third and much smaller group of men came to the mines as newly arrived immigrants. Most of them came from agricultural backgrounds and had no family tradition as miners. They did not choose to become miners but found no other type of work open to them.

I was born in Italy and came to America when I was 16. I was in Chicago looking for jobs, but no find. People there was put out of homes because they couldn't pay no rent, so I know I couldn't get job. I went down in the coal mine because that was all there was for me. My whole life I spend there, nothing else to do but work in mine.

I came from Austria. Nothing for immigrants but mines.

When I came over here I had no food, clothes, place to stay and keep warm. Only place I can find work is in the mine. I just stay there.

It appears that the men of each of these three groups became miners as a consequence of a limited field of occupational choices. A job in the mines seemed to be the only possible employment or the best among a few alternatives. This perhaps was the initial meaning which work as a miner had to these men.

The median age at which these men had begun work as miners was 17 years. They had left school at the median age of 14 years. The difference between these ages seems to represent a period of trying-out at various types of work—on the farm, on the railroad, as an apprentice at a trade—before settling into a job as a miner. For some, particularly the sons of miners, there was no trial period; but others, the sons of farmers or laborers, who came into the mines at a later average age, had had a short and usually varied experience at other types of work.

---

new employment; many boys undoubtedly entered the mines as a consequence of this local "boom" atmosphere.

Job Mobility

Once employed as miners, the men were remarkably immobile; less than one-fourth had worked thereafter for as much as a year in another occupation. Although some had done other types of work, the circumstances make it apparent that they had not in reality changed occupations.

After the mine closed down, I got a job at the packing house. Then the war come along, and they were needing men out at the mine, so I got on, and I'm still working there.

I worked on a construction gang once for seven months when the mine wasn't working, but I always been in the mines besides that.

I began mining when I was 16, and I've been at it ever since except for three years during the first World War. Then there was a time we went on strike for six months, so I went to Detroit and got a job.

I worked in a factory once for a while when the mines quit, but I hated that. Too much noise and confusion.

In contrast to this lack of interoccupational mobility, movement from mine to mine and from job to job within the same mine was very common. Few had worked continuously at the same place or at the same type of job.

I've been working in a mine for fifty-two years. I worked at trapping and loading, and I ran a cutting machine. I guess I worked at twenty-nine or thirty different places.

I started out mining fifty-four years ago, and I have been a trapper boy, mule-driver, machine operator, boss, examiner, and machine loader.

A part of this shifting from job to job was a result of changes in mining technology by which some types of work were rendered obsolete and new types created.

Mechanization

When these men first entered the mines as youths, the technology of mining could be described in the phrase, "a pick and a shovel, a man and a mule." One by one, machines were introduced which speeded production and lessened the physical demands upon the worker. Mechanization increased continuously from 1910 to the end of the second World War. Today all the basic operations involve the use of heavy, semiautomatic machinery. This technological revolution was vividly depicted in interviews.

I've done a little of everything in the mines. Thirty-three years is a long spell. Back in the hand loading days, I was a loader, and that was really work. I've been a shooter for several years. We first used powder for blasting, but now we have airdox [high-pressure air cartridges].

When they had horses and mules in the mines, I drove them a while, and I did hand loading. That was the hardest work of any.

I started out shooting with powder back in 1911. Now I operate a cutting machine, and I have a seat to sit on and operate the levers. That's the way mining came up.

They've come a long way in the coal mines since I started. All there used to be to coal-mining was a pick and shovel and some powder to shoot with. Now, everything is done by machines.

When I started to work in the mines forty-five years ago, we dug coal with a pick and pulled it to the bottom of the shaft. We used blasting powder and dug with a pick. Today it's all mechanized. Everything is in a rush today with the machines.

They have a lot of machines now, and it's easier than it used to be, but it's still hard work.

Although the physical strenuousness of labor has been greatly reduced, mechanization has not seemed an unmixed blessing, for it has been accompanied by a reduction in the number of jobs and a speeding-up of production.

Mechanization has sure taken a lot of jobs away from the men. Before we got loading machines and cutting machines, we had about 2,200 men on the payroll, but now there are only about 1,100. Machines increase production, but they sure take jobs.

At one time there were 900 men in the mine, but now we've got better machines, so it takes less to operate. Today, it takes only about 500 men to do the same job in a more efficient way.

When I start, I was young and strong, and me and my uncle load lots of coal. Coal-mining is not so hard now as when I start, but many men don't work because of the machines. Before machinery, lots of men make money. I like better today if more men work.

Greater speed was considered a handicap by some men, especially those of the oldest age level and those who had a physical disability:

In mining today every man has to do his job fast like a production line. I'm not fast enough to keep up with this modern machinery. In the days of hand mining, older men could still be working, but today the machines cut them out because they aren't fast enough.

It used to be an old man could go and take his time and make a small day's wages, anyway. But now, every man has a job to do where he is expected to hold up his end, and that gets hard on an old man when he has to go along with these young fellows. Most old men have worked in bad air, and that tells on you when you get older. Like me, I got no wind.

The requirements of the job the miner does now are vastly different from those of the job in which he first began. Undoubtedly, to many men, the lessened physical labor has made their present jobs seem "easy" and thus more desirable.[9] There is in this respect less reason to want to leave the job today than in the earlier period.

Accident and Injury

The frequency of injury and death among miners is well known.[10] These men had worked as miners an average of nearly forty years; all had witnessed accidents in which fellow-workers were injured or killed, and many had been injured themselves.

We had fourteen men killed in two weeks' time. Fourteen in two weeks! I guess that's the most we ever had in so short a time. In the thirty-three years I've worked in the mines, I've helped carry out 162 men.

I saw my buddy get burned up. I don't ever want to see anything like that again. The powder he was carrying caught fire and set him on fire and burned him up before we could do anything. Another time I seen 'em bring a fellow out with one leg broke twice and the other three times. You could see bones stickin' out all over his leg.

9. Some of the men had been shifted to jobs which required less physical labor, and this enters into the opinion that the work is less strenuous. However, analysis of job classifications showed that the older men had *not* moved into less strenuous jobs; there was a tendency for the "easiest" jobs to be filled by younger men. There was an inverse relation between age and work as a machine operator, indicating that the "lever-pulling" jobs were filled by younger men.

10. In recent years the number of deaths among coal-miners has averaged about 1,000 annually, and the number of injuries resulting in loss of work about 40,000. Together, these numbers represent about one-tenth of the men employed as miners (*Bituminous Coal Annual, 1950*, p. 156).

I helped dig a fellow out after a cave-in, and for months after when I passed that spot it gave me cold chills. Then, my son helped dig some fellows out one night. He came home afterward all shaken up, and said that after what he saw happened to them, he was going to quit. He did quit, too, the next day, and never went back.

There were four of us in a room setting timbers when all at once they started cracking, and we knew there was going to be a cave-in. All of us rushed for the opening, but me and my buddy were the only ones who made it. The others were killed.

Some of those who had been personally injured suffered no lasting effects, but others had been permanently disabled:

I've had maybe thirty-five to forty injuries, mostly small ones. But some of them did leave pretty good scars for me to remember them by.

I got my hand cut off, so they gave me a job as examiner.

I had so many accidents I couldn't count 'em. Got three ribs broke, a leg broke with a rock, and my fingers broke. And I even think I died once. I was in an explosion and all the air was gone. I stopped breathing and fell down, and some fellow dragged me out on my face.

I been in six explosions. Got banged up pretty bad and burned, too, but I'm still working.

I came pert near gettin' killed. A chunk of coal fell off the machine and broke a bone in my head. Then, here about two years ago, I got my back broken. Three vertebraes fractured.

These experiences of personal injury or of witnessing the injury of others become part of the meaning which the work of the miner takes on through the years and become a bond between him and others who have been involved in the same or similar situations.

In view of the constant possibility of personal injury, it is of interest to learn what adjustments were made by men who had continued to work under these conditions year after year.

I was there when they lost thirty-six men in a cave-in. Of course, you always know people are going to die, maybe the man next to you. You don't give it much thought. And a couple of days after they're dead, you don't think about it any more. They just kind of slip out of your mind.

Somebody left a switch open, and this fellow got caught between the cars. It just smashed him. Coal-mining's like that, though.

You get used to it, and it's just second nature to be careful. It don't ever worry me none at all.

I believe that on the day you're born the Maker knows just how you're goin' to leave this world. When you're supposed to go, you'll go, and that's all there is to it. I used to be afraid when I first started to work, but then I got to thinkin' about it. If I'm supposed to go while I'm in the mines, that's the way it'll be, and there's not much I can do about it.

Fully recognizing the dangers of their work, they had come to accept them as a matter of course. Whatever their initial anxieties may have been, most men had succeeded in rationalizing and philosophizing to the point at which danger seemed normal; but it is doubtful if it is ever completely forgotten.

More subtle and often more severe than direct physical injury is the effect of mine dust upon the lungs. The problems of underground ventilation have become particularly difficult since the introduction of high-speed cutting machines. The results are evident in these statements:

I was a machine man, and that started the trouble. The dust sprayed back and hurt my lungs. I had to have X-rays. See, here they are. You can see where the dust collected, and the hole in the lung.

With those machines now, they're dusty if you work on them, and at night you can't eat and spit up black stuff.

I've got asthma in what's called the critical stage.

The doc says not to work, but I tell him I have to when I'm able. Course, I well today, maybe sick tomorrow.

Presumably all miners recognize this threat to their health; the question is why they continue to work in spite of it. The reason in part is that the disorders develop gradually. Health may be unaffected for many years; then "asthma" begins, and a visit to the doctor brings personal realization of what had been merely possible. Often near the end of his work career the miner's work appears to him in the new perspective of its devastating effects upon his health. One man thus afflicted summed up the attitude of many in these words: "If I could do it again, I wouldn't go near the mines."

Work-Group Relations

Close co-ordination of activities is necessary in many types of work. Often it is essential, as in construction work, simply in order that the work of each individual may proceed without interruption. In mining there is the additional necessity that each worker observe the rules of safety which previous tragedies have shown to be essential to individual and collective survival. A strong feeling of interdependence and of responsibility for each other's welfare was evident in many interviews.

I was a mine examiner, and I had a great deal of responsibility. I was continually worrying about the men whose lives were dependent upon my wrong or right decisions. I realized that if I made a slip it might cost some of their lives.

I have to keep the power coming to the ventilators, or the air would stop circulating. That happened once, and they had to take all the trolleys loose from the motors to get the men out. If we'd left them on, the way they spark, there'd have been an explosion sure. The boss said, "Boys, don't anybody strike a match between here and the shaft, or none of us will get out alive."

A thoughtless act may endanger many lives. The following statement illustrates a typical effort to subordinate a new employee to the system of safety controls.

The foreman gave me a boy to watch over. I told him to go get something in another room. Well, I waited for a while for him to come back, but he didn't show up. I found him in the other room sitting on top of a pile of rock smoking a cigarette. I got him down and really gave him hell about that. No telling how much gas was in there.

To be an old-timer in the mines means something more than merely knowing the technique of a particular job; it also means awareness and acceptance of the responsibility which each man has for his fellow-workers. The sense of interdependence in relation to common dangers is undoubtedly an important factor in the spirit of solidarity which has characterized miners in all countries for many generations.

The Role of the Union

To most Illinois miners "union" means United Mine Workers of America, of which the men of this study group were members.[11] In terms of local officials, meetings, dues check-offs, strikes, safety regulations, and national leadership, the union is a concrete reality. A discussion of work experience would be incomplete without attention to the role of the union in effecting changes in wages, working conditions, and company policies.

Statements such as these were heard many times:

I joined the UMW in 1897, when it was in its infancy, and I am still a member. At first, they were pretty weak and didn't do much for the miners, but as the years went by, they gained strength through the fact that they could negotiate contracts and the miners by themselves couldn't.

I've belonged to the union ever since it was first organized in the mines around here. It has been a mighty fine thing, and I sure don't know what we would have done without it.

The union has often wielded its power through strikes of long duration. To the men in the mines, strikes have sometimes meant severe hardship through loss of income; but they have also frequently resulted in more advantageous pay scales and safety regulations. There is divided opinion regarding the values of striking.

I'm a union man, and I think the strikes have helped the miner's cause. In the long run, they have increased his rate of pay and lessened the danger of working in the mines.

Before the union came in, if you went on strike, the company brought in scabs to work or fired you or any other method to make you give in. Through the union, we have got better relations with the company, eight-hour shifts, good wages, a retirement plan, benefits for injuries, and a hospital plan.

Some men held opposite opinions:

Strikes are useless, not only because they cost the miners and the company money, through loss of time and production, but also because they always come back to a negotiation board to be settled. If the union and the company officials sat down and tried to reach a settlement, strikes could be avoided.

I never agitated or took any active part in strikes. There have been strikes that I didn't approve of, but that is not for me to say. Most of us would have liked to go on working, but we did as the rest did.

11. Illinois has been one of the strongholds of miners' unions since 1861. See Edward A. Wieck, *The American Miner's Association* (New York: Russell Sage Foundation, 1940), and McAlister Coleman, *Men and Coal* (New York: Farrar & Rinehart, 1943).

Apart from the issue of strikes, however, there was general agreement concerning the benefits of unionism. The great majority of men subscribed to the following opinions:

The miners support and believe in the union. If it weren't for the union, we wouldn't have anything.

The union has won for us everything that we have. The company wouldn't give us a damn thing without it.

In addition to its specific achievements in contracts with the operators, the union has played another and perhaps equally important function: it has provided a set of common experiences and purposes. For more than thirty years miners have found a dynamic symbol in the figure of John L. Lewis. In the thinking of many miners, all that is good or bad, won or lost, in the actions of the union is attributed to Lewis personally.

Coal-mining's come a long way since I started, and if you ask me, it's the union that's responsible for the improvements. Now, I'm not one of these boys that thinks John L.'s a little god—he's got his faults, and plenty of 'em—but he's done a lot for us. You got to admit that.

John L.'s union is the best there is. He's got us mine laws and started the pension and did a lot of good.

I think this holds true of almost every miner. I don't approve of all John L.'s policies, but old John is the boy for us.

I'm a 100 per cent union man. I admire John L. Lewis, and I don't care what other people think of him.

There are some dissenters:

Two years ago that damn John L. made us strike and bring on a shortage of coal, while everyone was freezing. None of us coal-miners has got too much money, and it was pretty hard sledding, and lots of us went in debt. If he expects us miners to starve and freeze, then he should have to, too. He ain't no better than us. I think a lot of the union, but not much of him; he ain't really done anything to help us.

I'd get my head chopped off if I said this around the mine, but I don't like John L. Lewis. He does a lot of good, but he's almost a one-man dictator. I don't believe in one man having so much power.

The job of the miner in the past generation would not have had the same meaning had Lewis not risen to leadership of the union; it will not be the same in his absence. He has approached nearer the role of the folk hero than any leader in the history of the American labor movement, and to that extent he has affected the miners' conceptions of themselves, their status, and their work.

MEANINGS OF WORK

The preceding sections have indicated something of the complexity of the individual worker's job-related experiences. This section is concerned with the predominant meanings which the miner's work activity has assumed, from his own point of view, in the course of a long career.

The technique was as follows. Well along in the course of the interview, the interviewer asked what meaning the subject's work had had for him. The usual response to this question was a request for an explanation. The interviewer then read a set of prepared statements said to have been made by "other workers" and asked the subject to indicate which of these best represented his own feelings; the statements were repeated as often as necessary, and the interviewer refrained from suggesting a choice.[12] The nature of the statements will become apparent in the following paragraphs.

The results are given in Table 9, where the categories are the same as those described in chapter i and used in the other studies. As the table indicates, 18 per cent of the men said that their work had no other meaning to them than the money it provided. Another 69 per cent recognized the financial meaning of work but placed one of the extra-economic meanings ahead of it in importance. This left 13 per cent who did not mention earning a living as a significant meaning of the job.

Men included in the first group, who recognized only a financial meaning in work, gave statements of this nature:

Mining is no pleasure. It hasn't meant anything more to me than a living.

12. Complete standardization of the form of the question was not attempted. Interviewers were instructed to adhere to one of the following: "A man who has worked as long as you have as a miner must have a pretty clear idea of what his work means to him—what would you say your work means to you?" "We have been asking other miners what meaning their work has to them—can you tell me what meaning your work has to you?" The statements read in explanation of the question had been developed from interviews conducted with other work groups, as described in other chapters of this volume, and were directly adopted for this study to facilitate comparison.

I'll tell ya the truth, I haven't seen a day I enjoyed my work. Ya work for what ya can get out of it. I know a fellow who says the secret of a long life is hard work, but he ain't work a day in sixteen years.

Outside of the money I get, my work doesn't mean anything—nothing!

It means an income, and that's all!

Statements of this type represent an extreme degree of pecuniary emphasis. These men did not discuss or acknowledge any

TABLE 9

TYPES OF PERSONAL MEANINGS OF WORK: COAL-MINERS

Statements Presented in Interviews	No.	Per Cent
1. Work has no meaning other than the wages it provides.	27	17.5
2. Work has filled my day and given me something to do.	29	19
3, *a* and *b*. Work has given me self-respect and the respect of others.	27	17.5
4. Work has given me a chance to be with and work with others.	29	19
5, *a* and *c*. Work has been a source of new and interesting experiences.	17	11
5, *d*. Work has given me a chance to be useful.	24	16
Total.	153*	100.0

* In 33 interviews out of 186, the questions and explanations were not understood, and no response was recorded: these men were mainly of foreign birth, a group which other phases of the study indicated to hold attitudes toward work as primarily a means of making a living.

meanings other than income connected with their work; they viewed work as entirely instrumental rather than intrinsically meaningful.

Turning now to the other responses in Table 9, it is seen that more than four-fifths of the men attributed inherent meanings of some nature to their work.

Many men designated more than one of the statements as applicable to their experience; the replies shown in Table 9 are those which they designated as the most important to them. Thus, the total frequency of mention of these factors was actually greater than the table indicates. The following comments pertain only to the major extra-economic meanings of work.

There was no marked tendency to concentrate upon any one of the statements. The meanings of association with fellow-workers and of work as a time-filling, activity-giving task were equally emphasized; status or self-respect and the feeling of usefulness were mentioned only slightly less often. The differences in rank order among these four statements is slight and probably without significance. However, attention should be called to the number of men who stated that their work gave them "something to do"; the value placed upon sheer routine activity may be easily overlooked. In a later discussion of attitudes toward retirement it will be seen that this is a basic meaning of work to men of certain circumstances and temperament.

The statement which was least frequently chosen concerned work as a source of new and interesting experiences. Two factors perhaps jointly account for this: (1) the long average work career, involving familiarization with virtually all phases of the industry, and (2) the relatively unchanging physical environment of the job and the stable constitution of the work group. On the other hand, the men who stated that their work was meaningful because of new experiences usually indicated that they had in mind changes to a different work group or shift; in other words, changes of personalities rather than of technology.

As a parallel to the statements previously quoted from men who looked upon work entirely as a means of earning a living, it is appropriate to cite a few of the remarks made by men who emphasized the extra-economic meanings of their work.

What has my work meant to me? Well, it's kept me busy and given me a lot to think about. More important than that, though, it has enabled me to fulfil one of my strongest beliefs. I've always felt that every person owed a debt to society and needed to contribute something, or they had missed their purpose in being put on earth.

In the mine you're on your own and you do your job to suit yourself. You're your own boss. The foreman knows you can do your job, and that kind of situation just calls you back.

I enjoy my job, and I'm glad to talk about it. I got into mining accidentally. I wanted to be a farmer when I was a kid, but there was a chance to drive mules in the mine. It paid me a little money, but mainly it made me feel important. Well, I still think my job's important, even if it doesn't pay too much. There isn't a better bunch nowhere than the fellows I work with.

Somehow when you get into the mining and you like the men you work with, you just get to the place after while that you don't want to leave. Once that fever gets hold of a man, he'll never be good for anything else.

A fellow may quit the mines, but when they whistle, he goes back. I've had a lot better jobs, but I've always liked to work in the mines. I can't explain it, except I like being with the gang; I never could just sit around much.

These statements represent views which are essentially independent of considerations of income from work. They may be paraphrased somewhat as follows: A man can earn a living at any of several types of work, but the kinds of meanings expressed here are found only in jobs and work groups of the sort in which these men were involved. Money is money regardless of its source in this job situation or that; but friendship, respect, and a sense of usefulness arise within the context of their specific job situation. For only one segment of the group is an exception to this statement necessary: those who found their work meaningful merely by reason of its routine nature. As will appear in a later section, work to these men is not merely a cornerstone but rather the foundation of personal life-organization.

Rising Wages and Living Standards

The earnings of miners have risen more sharply than those of other workers within the last twenty years, having more than doubled within the past decade. But even this increase is less impressive than that which occurred in the experience of most of these men.[13]

When I was just 14, I was working ten hours a day for 75 cents. That was 75 cents a day, not an hour, too.

When I started mining in 1908, I worked for $1.13 a day. I loaded coal for 38 cents a ton.

13. For a detailed table of wages for various mining jobs in 1899 see *United Mine Workers Journal*, Vol. LXII, No. 12 (June 15, 1951). The pay scale established by contract in 1950 provided basic rates ranging from $15 to $21 per day for various types of work. Actual hourly earnings for Illinois miners averaged $2.28, and average employment was 33.9 hours in March, 1951 (*Illinois Labor Bulletin*, XI [May–June, 1951], 17).

Back in 1910, when I was starting out, I worked for union wages, but you can guess what the rates were. I got about a dollar a day. Now I've been raised to $18 a day.

The median wage at present is approximately $18 per day. But annual income falls far short of the level which the daily rate suggests, for the mines do not work more than three days out of five on the average, and in the summer months there is nearly complete shutdown. Thus arises one of the severe problems of the industry, and with it a perennial complaint of the miners:[14]

The miners were working good until about 1925, but then we began getting only about two days each pay. For a while we got only four days a month at $5.37 a day. Believe me, it's damn hard raising a family on less than a dollar a day.

You work good for a couple of months and then are off or have bad work the rest of the year. You have to spend all you save and then go in debt. You never get out of debt.

We make good money when we work. I make over $16 a day. But maybe we don't get over one or two days a week.

Mining's too uncertain. Here's what I mean. I draw top wages at the mine. There's only sixteen men in my kind of job. And we make $97 for a six-day week. But we never get that. I haven't worked six days a week for two years. Last year we only went down 153 days. This year's even worse so far.

Sure, it pays good by the day, but in winter you eat pork chops and in summer you eat grass.

During the second World War, when the mines worked more days per year than ever in their history, the annual wages were correspondingly high. Many men paid off debts and mortgages or increased their savings; others invested in the remodeling of their homes and purchased furniture and automobiles. The positive effect upon their feelings of status in the community was quite apparent.

14. Since 1910 the trend in number of days worked has been downward. Men who originally came into full-time jobs have found their jobs reduced to little more than half-time. Some men erroneously believe that this reduction is due to "the coal playing out," which is far from true, as the local reserves are very great. The majority recognize that it is due to the greater productivity of mechanized mines and to the inroads upon coal consumption which have been made by other sources of energy, particularly gas and oil.

Since we been gettin' more pay, seems like people think more of us than they used to. Miners can afford better houses than they used to.

My home is all paid for now. It is nicer than many in town, and it makes me feel that I have been able to get something that not everyone else has.

The public has come to have a higher regard for miners now. We don't have to work as hard as we did before we got all these machines, and we get more money, too. We can drive around in a new car and live in a nice house just like anybody else.

Some men took great pride in showing interviewers the improvements they had been able to make in their homes.

I don't owe a cent on the house now. I got my roof fixed two years ago. I had two years to pay it off, and I've done paid it off already. When I first started out in the mines, you really had to have a good day to make $3.50 a day. Now, I make $18.17 a day. You can't have electric stoves on $3.50 a day. Yes, sir, I've got an electric stove. Come in here, I'll show you. See, there's the bathroom. Sure cost me a lot to get that put in. Here, we fixed up the back porch; big enough for a person to sleep in. In here, we fixed up the kitchen. Over there is the electric stove. I've got an electric clock, a toaster, washer, a doorbell, and everything electric you could imagine. You couldn't do that on $3.50 a day.

Come on, I'll show you the house. This sure is a nice kitchen. The missus likes it. She got me to fix it up the first of any rooms because she said she would spend most of her time here, and, by golly, she does. It isn't much, but it's pretty good for poor folks, don't you think?

The advance in living standards which these statements represent is not likely to be lost short of a general economic depression. An adequate account of the meaning of work to these men must necessarily include reference to the increase in real wages which most of them have experienced. And, as in the case of lessened physical exertion resulting from mechanization, the benefits of a high pay scale may increase reluctance to leave the job upon reaching the age of retirement.

Social Status and Self-conceptions

The meaning of work-related activities arises partly through consciousness of the manner in which they are defined by others. In personal interaction within and without the community and through media of mass communication the individual encounters the evaluations which others make of his personal qualities, his occupation, and his group affiliations. This section is concerned with the miner's awareness of and reaction to the attitudes of others toward him in the role of coal-miner and union member.

An approach to the existence of differential attitudes toward miners was made through an interview question which asked the subject whether he felt that "miners are a separate group in this community." Each of these typical replies refers to a different town:

No, there are no differences around here. Just one town, all the same sort of people.

No, I don't think the community thinks of the miner as a separate class. Most of us are miners here, and we look upon it as a good kind of job. All of this town is a working class of people, and we think all of us are about the same.

The miners just mix and mingle with all the rest. Everybody seems to get along here, and nobody tries to high-hat the rest very much.

I don't think miners are classed as a special group. Sure, there's a few cake-eaters, but more people remember that the town was built up by miners, and they respect us for that.

The percentage of employed males working as miners in the various towns ranges from 28 to 50; in only one of the smallest towns does it exceed the latter figure. Numerically, they are a minority occupational group, yet it seems clear that they do not feel that they are stereotyped as a group and subjected to categorical treatment. As individuals, they recognize differences in status, as between themselves and managers and professionals, for example; but they do not think of themselves as different from other "workingmen." Their work does not carry for them the meaning of a segregative activity within their home communities.[15]

Their feelings concerning the manner in which their occupa-

15. Among the factors limiting the rise of categorical contacts within the community are the following: the small size of the communities and the resulting high degree of personal acquaintance; the absence of a traditional upper class; the local origin of the majority of miners and their cultural and kinship affinities with the rest of the populace; the dispersion of miners' homes throughout the residential areas; and the relatively high income of miners in comparison with white-collar workers and other industrial workers.

tion is viewed by persons outside the local communities "who don't know what we are really like" follow a very different pattern. Rather than feeling that they are accepted, they feel that "outsiders" look down upon them and have a low opinion of their work.

Once in a while someone will say we are in a dirty industry and that we never get all of the dirt washed away. But here where most men work in the mines you couldn't expect that we'd be looked down upon. Up in Gary where my daughter lives, it is a different story. Miners just aren't no good in their minds. Of course, I don't think those steelworkers are so hot, either.

People that aren't around the coal mines think there's just a bunch of little foreigners working in them. When we were up in Bloomington on vacation I was standing on a street corner and got in a conversation with a farmer. He started talking about the miners down in southern Illinois, saying he would like to see some of them sometimes, just to see what they looked like. I told him I was a coal-miner, and was he surprised! He even called his daughter over so she could get a look at me. I got kind of tickled about that. Those people ought to get around a little more. They'd find out that coal-miners are really a nice bunch of folks.

A usual reaction to the depreciatory attitude of outsiders is one of rejection or of tolerant amusement; it does not significantly alter the feeling of acceptance engendered by experience within the local community. There is an exception to this, however, which is probably of increasing importance, namely, the reaction to public opinion as conveyed by press and radio, particularly with regard to the efforts of the union to obtain better wages and working conditions through strikes. The following statements indicate marked sensitivity to public opinion relating to the frequent strikes.

People are always looking down on miners. Every time we have a strike, radio commentators all yell we're wrong. They don't know anything about it. Last time we struck one of them said the company should just take us and shove us down the shaft if we didn't get back to work. I turned that stuff off the minute I heard it. People don't know how many men get killed in the mines. We have to strike sometimes to get better conditions.

I don't like to strike, because people all get mad at the miners then. I wish the people would realize that the miner has to live too, and not hate him when he tries to better conditions for himself. It bothers me the way people say bad things about the miners, and makes me ashamed of my job.

People don't know much about the union, but they understand that it's necessary for miners. There are some that fight the unions, but most people like them. There is one newspaper that tries to make us out to be different because of our occupation and our union. We just don't buy or read that paper any more, although it would be a good thing to get both sides of the story. If we read what the paper said against us, we would be able to defend ourselves better.

The picture of strike activities and of public reaction which is presented by mass media seems to be viewed skeptically by many miners. If a distortion is recognized or when a sense of injustice is aroused, a new bond of sympathy arises among fellow-workers. The tense and defamatory publicity which has often surrounded strikes seemingly has created a feeling that the miners' situation and purposes are misrepresented and misunderstood.[16] A majority of the men believed their jobs were better jobs because of the changes in wages and working conditions attained through strikes.

Pride in the Job

Pride is a personal sentiment which directly or indirectly reflects the good opinion of others. As a response to specific circumstances it contributes to the more generalized feeling of self-respect. In Table 9 it was indicated that self-respect was an important meaning of work to many men of this group. It is the purpose of this section to illustrate some of the sources of self-respect in the specific feelings of pride which develop in the course of the miners' work.

16. If mass media have been used to drive a wedge between union members and leadership, as some labor leaders and economists believe, the actual effect upon the miners seems to have been to create a greater sense of solidarity; certainly conflict serves this function in many kinds of group relationships. During the strikes of 1950 many miners in the area were skeptical of press releases reporting the "weakening" of miners in other parts of the country (cf. W. E. Moore, *Industrial Relations and the Social Order* [New York: Macmillan Co., 1951], esp. pp. 365–66, and E. W. Bakke and Clark Kerr, *Unions, Management and the Public* [New York: Harcourt, Brace & Co., 1948], Parts 14 and 27). It is not intended to intimate that miners usually have a strong sense of *esprit de corps* as union members; ordinarily they are "job-conscious" and look upon the union as an instrument for protecting and bettering their jobs. Conflict brings a shift toward ideological principles.

An intriguing feature of the data obtained in interviews was the number and variety of types of pride in the job expressed by these men. Some were mentioned by many men; others by only one or a few. This presentation is necessarily limited to one or two examples of each type; they are listed roughly in order of decreasing frequency.

1. *Responsibility for welfare of others:*

I am very proud of my job because I examine the mine to make sure it is safe. I save a lot of men by taking chances for them.

The responsibility of a job like mine makes you feel your worth. Every man depends on the others for the safety of the whole crew. When we had nine hundred men working, all their lives were in my hands, and we never had an accident. That's the kind of thing that makes you proud of being able to do your job.

2. *Individual selection for a particular job:*

My job was especially created for me.

Out of six hundred men in the mine, they picked me for this job.

3. *Skill in a specialized type of work:*

This job I've got of drillin' and shootin' is the most particular job. You've got to know your business.

There are some jobs a man can do after it's once showed to him, but a machine man has to know something special.

4. *Key position upon which work of others depends:*

I had no special kind of training for my job, but I think it's pretty important. The mine moves when the motorman moves, and I do the moving. I'll never be decorated by the President because of it, but there's pride in a job when it's well done.

5. *Unusual achievement and recognition:*

I helped to hoist the world's record once, and I'll never stop feeling good about it. The company gave us certificates of honor for that, and it's a feat to be proud of. You feel good when you achieve something like that.

6. *Accumulated experience and general knowledge:*

When I lost my job about two years ago, I went over to the mine, but they told me if I was over 57 they didn't want me. But then they found out how much experience I had and that I knew my work well, so they sent for me. That just shows how important experience is. They need good men.

7. *Reputation for faithfulness and hard work:*

I'm known as one of the hardest-working miners around here. It makes me tired, but I like to feel that I do my part.

I've worked for the same company almost thirty years. If a man does good work, he doesn't have any trouble keeping a job.

8. *Conformity and avoidance of conflict:*

I've worked in the mines for forty-five years, and in all that time I've never had a boss call me down for anything.

Six of us work side by side every day, and we work as a team. We ain't had a cross word or falling-out in nine years, and, believe me, that keeps accidents down.

9. *Ability to control others:*

The men always want to do a good job for me. They always ask me how they did after a certain job, and they really beam when I praise them. You've got to use psychology in the mines. I've had men say they can't do any good without me. They say just my being there keeps things rolling.

These were the major sources of self-respect described in interviews.[17] It will be noted that they pertain primarily to work situations and to the opinions of fellow-workers. They do not reflect a sense of prestige in the eyes of the community or society at large. They do not involve comparisons with other kinds of work; there is no indication of a feeling that the general character of the occupation commands respect.[18] The circumstances which contribute to feelings of pride seem to be those of the job itself. There was no mention of feelings of pride arising from the opinions of family, neighbors, or associates; the reference group was the work group. Only when speaking of the material standard of living purchased through wages did the feeling of pride encompass a larger group. It can only be inferred that other groups do not pro-

17. A number of other circumstances were mentioned by one or two men: ability to do an especially difficult job; length of work with the same company; publicity by company magazine because of age or years worked without accident; etc. Important as these were to individuals, they did not represent common sentiments.

18. Historically, mining has never carried prestige; yet prior to the present century it was looked upon as a craft involving training and skill, as indicated in the old term "practical miner" and in the continuing, somewhat archaic, system of official certification and licensing.

vide occasions for the development of pride in occupation. Possibly there is an awareness of a decline in the prestige of the occupation which was not adequately brought out in interviews; some evidence bearing upon this is presented in the following pages.

This discussion would be incomplete without mention of the small minority of men who had never found in their jobs any effective occasions for the development of feelings of pride. They made statements of this nature:

> Why would anyone be proud of being a miner? I'm not. I just have to have money to live on, and I can't do anything else. I'd like to get an easier job, but there aren't any easy jobs in the mines.

> My job is hard work, but it's not important. If I go, someone else will do it. There's no future in the mines. The company doesn't care anything about us. Just get out the coal, get out the coal. They don't care for us. I don't have any gripes, especially; I just do my job and leave and come home.

How far these statements represent merely exceptional personality attributes or more general unspoken feelings cannot be determined. A more detailed inquiry might have shown them to be a common pattern among the men to whom work has the meaning of an instrumental activity only.

In summary, it appears that the pride of these men in their jobs and the self-respect to which it contributes is rather sharply restricted in three ways, namely, as to source, intensity, and frequency. It is largely limited to the work group; it is most often expressed incidentally in connection with other matters; and certainly it is not characteristic of the group. Finally, those to whom self-respect is an important meaning of work show no consensus as to the feature of their work which occasions pride. There seem to be no common denominators of experience within the mine or the community except the negative ones of common exposure to hazards of the job and to the instability of the industry.

Mining as a Career for Youth

An indirect but useful method for discovering the esteem which an individual attaches to his job is to ask whether he would wish others with whom he has close personal relationships to undergo the same kinds of experiences. As his retrospective evaluation of his own experiences is negative or positive, so presumably would he caution others against following similar paths or encourage them to do so. The men of this group were asked whether they would "advise a young man to take up mining as a career." Although the question was stated in general terms, nearly every man assumed that it referred to the members of his own family or to those of his friends. The responses pertained mainly to sons, sons-in-law, or sons of neighbors. They gave a revealing picture of the man's evaluations of his own experiences and provided important insights concerning the meaning of work which were not obtained in any other manner.

The replies were overwhelmingly negative; there were no unqualified affirmative replies. They followed four major patterns: mining is too hard and too dangerous; it does not provide steady work or adequate income; the opportunities for employment in the industry are constantly decreasing; and many more desirable occupations are available and should be taken advantage of.[19] These themes were interwoven in the thinking of most men. This statement by a miner of forty-three years' experience is representative:

No, I wouldn't advise a young man to go into mining. Mainly because it's a hard life. There's no certainty about it; it's either a feast or a famine. You may work good for a while, then you may starve for a while. I've got three boys, and I steered them clear of mining because I didn't want them to have to live the life I've had to live. If a fellow could get into a job of managing, I don't guess it would be such a bad life. But the ordinary miner don't mean much. If you're killed, why, there's always another man to take your place. Life gets pretty cheap.

The various themes were dealt with more specifically in the following manner:

I've never wanted my sons to become miners because the work is so dangerous and very hard. I'm glad they stayed out of the mines.

I wouldn't advise a young man to go into the mines. It is too dangerous. Our neighbors sent their boy to me the other day to see if I would get him a job where I work. I wouldn't do it. I didn't want him to go into the mines and get killed.

19. Compare the informative discussion of similar views among British miners presented by A. J. Jaffe and Charles D. Stewart, *Manpower Resources and Utilization* (New York: John Wiley & Sons, 1951), pp. 392–95.

I wouldn't advise a young man to go into the coal mines unless I had something against him. The work is not steady enough.

There's no future in the mines. There won't be much more work unless there is a war, and we don't want that. Electricity, gas, and oil have cut down the use of coal. The youth should stay out of the coal mines.

My boy got a job in St. Louis, and I sure am glad. There's too many things a young fellow can get into nowadays—radio, television, air conditioning, and the like. There's no future in mining for a young guy.

Mining is like a disease; I don't want my boys to have it. They've all gotten jobs elsewhere, and I'm sure they are better off where they are. I don't know why a young man would want a job in the mines.

My older son worked as a miner for three months but didn't like it and quit, and I was glad. The youngest hasn't done any mining. He went to law school and passed his bar exam and started practicing law here.

These statements indicate quite clearly the determined reaction of the fathers to a repetition of their own careers by their sons. It appears that the sons do not escape from a family tradition of mining; they are pushed into a different mode of life.

All my family has been miners right up to my son. I always tried to keep him out of the mines. I wanted him to go to school, and he graduated from the University. We worked hard to get him through.

The ability of the fathers to pay part of the costs of vocational training or university education for their sons and thus perhaps to enable them to avoid the hardships of the fathers' occupation constitutes no small part of the meaning of work. Perhaps in a more profound sense than these statements reveal the fathers live vicariously in the attainments of their sons.

These paragraphs provide a background for the interpretation of Table 10. If the census classifications which the table utilizes are thought to represent a rough socioeconomic status scale, it is evident that about one-quarter of the sons had moved upward into occupations of higher status than their fathers'. The deviation from the occupations of the subjects' fathers is particularly striking: 55 per cent of the grandfathers were farmers, as compared with only 1 per cent of the grandsons. The major interest in the table in the present connection centers upon the fact that seven out of ten of the sons have not followed in the footsteps of their fathers. The miner-father–miner-son tradition has been maintained by only a small minority. Some of the reasons, the most important ones, it is believed, have been described here. In the long perspective of forty years' experience the occupation seems

TABLE 10

OCCUPATIONS OF SUBJECTS' SONS

Occupation of Son*	No.	Per Cent
Professional and semiprofessional workers........	7	3.8
Proprietors, managers, and officials, nonfarm....	11	6.0
Farmers and farm managers...................	2	1.1
Clerical, sales, and kindred workers...........	15	8.2
Craftsmen, foremen, and kindred workers.......	13	7.1
Operatives and kindred workers...............	85	46.4
Protective and service workers†..............	36	19.7
Laborers, except farm and mine..............	14	7.7
Total.................................	183	100.0
Coal-miners (included above as "Operatives")..	55	30.1

* Does not include 25 sons still in school, 6 unemployed, 7 deceased, and 19 occupations not reported.
† Includes 33 sons in military service.

too heavily weighted with hardships and insecurities. Their work has a meaning which the men express less well in words than in the act of directing their sons along a different path.[20]

ATTITUDES TOWARD RETIREMENT

One of the objectives of this study was to investigate the relationship between meanings of work and attitudes toward retirement. Retirement signifies the termination of one major life-role and the assumption of another, a transition from one status and kind of activity to others of different character. It is perhaps inevitably a personal crisis which calls for a more or less fundamental reorientation of attitudes, a necessity which is often anticipated but rarely welcomed. Retirement itself and the activities which follow it involve decisions which may have been long in

20. The failure of the occupational tradition which these data seem to indicate probably signifies the imminence of the same problems of recruiting a labor force which have plagued the industry in other countries (*ibid.*).

the making and are based, in part, upon an intricate structure of experiences and feelings such as has been described in the previous pages and, in part, upon the conceptions which the individual has of the nature and magnitude of the problems which will arise when he leaves his job.

The present interest in these problems is indicated by stating the major questions which are raised: How has the development of an industry-wide pension plan affected the willingness of miners to retire? Apart from the matter of income, how do they look upon the prospect of quitting their jobs? What do they expect to miss most when they leave their jobs? What do they look forward to in retirement, and what are they worried about? What plans have they made? The discussion is an extension of the previous consideration of the meanings of work, from which certain interpretations are derived, and which it is intended to supplement.

Effects of Miners' Pension

The payment of a monthly pension of $100 at age 60 to members of the UMWA who had been miners for twenty years became possible as a result of contract negotiations in 1947.[21] Financing of the system through royalties paid by operators on each ton of coal mined was a major issue in a series of work stoppages during the two preceding years. Pension payments began in 1948 but were suspended for eight months in 1949 and 1950 when disbursements threatened to exceed income by several million dollars; restitution of lost payments to the affected individuals was never made.[22] A nation-wide coal strike in January and February, 1950, resulted in increased royalty payments into the Welfare and Retirement Fund and a modification of the rules of eligibility. Pensions have been paid without interruption since March of that year.

The pension scheme was received by the miners with whole-

21. Other contract provisions regarding death benefits and hospitalization have no direct relevance to the present discussion.

22. The cessation of payments was due to an actual deficit; the reason for the deficit was not agreed upon. The union contended that the number of applications for the pension had greatly exceeded expectations; the operators contended that there were irregularities in the administration of the system.

hearted approval. Older miners, especially, reacted in the manner if not with the enthusiasm of the miner who received his first pension check at the hands of the union president with the exclamation, "Mr. Lewis, this is the greatest thing since Jesus Christ!"[23]

Fifteen years ago payments of $100 per month would have given an annual income one-third greater than a miner would have earned through working; at present, $1,200 represents less than half the average earnings. Few pension plans are designed to provide as much income in retirement as was earned during the working years. But many of these men had reached or were approaching the age of eligibility for retirement with continuing responsibilities for the support of minor children and other dependents which could be met only by maintaining current income. An additional complication is introduced by the steady rise in the cost of living, which has rendered both pension and accumulated savings less adequate than they seemed a few years earlier. It is not surprising, therefore, that many men made statements of the following sort:

That $100 won't go nowhere today; we couldn't live on that.

I'm not planning to retire because I see no way that my wife and I can live off $100 a month. With the cost of living so high now, I wouldn't think of quitting as long as I'm able to work.

The only reason I haven't retired now is that I want to try to make a little more money before I do. Everything has gone up so high a person needs a little money besides his pension in order to live.

Whether they could reduce their standards of living to the level which they believe the amount of the pension would require without real hardship is irrelevant to this discussion. The fact is that they feel, strongly, that they must continue to work, not to subsist, but to maintain the pattern of life which their families have developed through the years.[24]

Nearly all these men would be eligible to receive Social Secu-

23. Saul Alinsky, *John L. Lewis: An Unauthorized Biography* (New York: G. P. Putnam's Sons, 1949), p. 357.

24. Attempts to determine objectively how much income an individual or a family "needs" usually fail to take account of the subjective nature of needs, that is, of "felt needs"; and it is these which enter into the decision to retire or to continue working.

rity payments averaging perhaps $60 monthly upon reaching age 65. However, the difference of five years in age of eligibility for the miners' pension and for Social Security payments is an important factor affecting the intention to retire at age 60. It is evident in these statements:

I could get the pension now, but I've got two years to wait for Social Security. If I could get it now, I'd quit today.

If the Social Security was fixed so I could draw it now, I'd quit in a minute; but I can't draw it until I'm 65. Lots of fellows feel the same way about it.

I quit next year maybe. Can't get Social Security yet or I'd quit now. Just pension. Hell, I got home and family.

I would want to retire if the Social Security age was lowered. We could get the $100 plus Social Security, and then we could make it all right.

The significant fact here is that the prospect of a larger retirement income at age 65 than at age 60 is a major incentive to continue working during the intervening five years. The repeated statement, "I'd quit today if . . . ," together with the large number of men who are actually at work after age 60, leaves little doubt that the pension alone is deemed insufficient to meet the costs of living. Failure to retire at age 60 is not necessarily an indication of a desire to continue working. Work in the interim is essential to maintain income until current obligations have lessened, until health fails, or until the individual becomes willing to accept a decline in his standard of living.

A third and very important component of attitudes toward retirement is the widespread belief that the pension system does not actually guarantee income after retirement. This belief had its origin in the suspension of pension payments in September, 1949, when the pension fund was exhausted. Subsequently, the amount paid into the fund as royalties was increased; nevertheless, the adequacy of the fund depends upon the number of tons of coal mined, the number of pensioners, and the continuance of the contract provision for royalty payments.[25] The attitudes of the men toward these contingencies are clear.

25. "Under pension plans that are not guaranteed by an actuarially sound pension trust fund, workers never build up an equity and have no real security,

I don't think the pension will stand up. The miners are all scared of it. You know, the payments stopped there a while back, and the boys are all scared to retire now.

This contract-to-contract pension ain't no good. If I could be sure of it, I'd quit now, but I can't because if they'd stop it, I couldn't make out.

The pension is okay now while the mines are paying into the fund and only a few are getting it. When the mines quit paying, it can't last. They won't be able to pay either when a lot more men get on it, because they'll bankrupt the fund.

If I retire, the way our pension plan is now, a feller can't be sure just how long he can get it. If I retired and was countin' on my pension, they might just stop the whole thing just any time, and then where would I be? They ain't hirin' many men now, and with me bein' old as I am, it'd be pretty near impossible for me to get on again.

One additional consideration of this nature needs to be mentioned. At the time of a strike, which ordinarily signifies the termination of the existing contract, payments into the pension fund are stopped. If the strike is a long one, the fund may be depleted. Knowing the frequency and duration of strikes from long personal experience, the men are understandably skeptical of the effects which future strikes may have upon their own pensions when they retire.

The following conclusions may be drawn regarding the relation of the pension system to retirement at age 60: (1) the amount is thought to be insufficient to cover necessary expenditures; (2) a large proportion of the group state that, if Social Security payments were available in addition to the pension at age 60, they would prefer to retire; (3) many continue working beyond age 60 contrary to their wish to retire because of obligations to dependents which they believe cannot be met by pension payments alone; and (4) there is genuine distrust of the stability of the pension plan which causes many to continue to work

----

since they are forced to make the same fight for pensions at the end of each contract. The miners' pension plan is a good example. It is a 'pay as you go' plan, not guaranteed by an actuarially sound pension trust fund. Therefore the miners have been forced to fight for pensions and old-age security at the end of each contract" (Walter P. Reuther, "Practical Aims and Purposes of American Labor," *Annals of the American Academy of Political and Social Science*, CCLXXIV [March, 1951], 68).

rather than risk its possible breakdown. These factors operate to limit considerably the role which the pension plan plays in the decision of the individual to retire.

Quitting the Job

Retirement on pension at age 60 is presumably voluntary. Existing company-union contracts prohibit dismissal of a miner on the basis of age alone. In view of this policy it was pertinent to ask at what age the men of this group thought a man should retire. Of those who stated a specific age, 18 per cent designated ages 50 or 55; 45 per cent, age 60; and 36 per cent, ages 65 or 70.[26] Thus, more than three-fifths would have preferred to quit their jobs before or at age 60; yet all were actually at work, nearly half of them beyond age 60.

On the basis of what has been reported in the previous section, it might be assumed that those who had or who wished to continue to work beyond the retirement age were acting from economic motives, that is, to accumulate savings, provide for dependents, or maintain income until eligible for Social Security. The validity of the assumption is not self-evident, however. It is possible that an inquiry into the reasons for continuing work might reveal an important relationship between the extra-economic meanings of work and the actual or expected decisions of individual workers upon reaching retirement age.

A part of each interview concerned this problem. The individual was asked what he thought he would miss most about his job when he retired; the replies were categorized in approximately the same manner as those pertaining to meanings of work as described in an earlier section. The distribution of responses is shown in Table 11. As would be expected, the largest proportion, 51 per cent, stated that they would miss the income from their jobs. Later a question will be raised concerning the interpretation to be placed upon this reply; for the moment it may be merely noted as the most frequent response.

26. Not all the group were willing to specify an age for retirement: 25 per cent stated that retirement should be based upon consideration of individual circumstances, such as health, financial condition, ability to do a satisfactory day's work, etc. A frequent statement was that a man should be eligible for voluntary retirement on pension after a given length of service—thirty, forty, or fifty years—regardless of chronological age.

The statements by a few men that they would miss nothing about their jobs are of particular interest. They answered the question with sarcasm or irony:

I won't miss anything about that job—absolutely nothing.

I'll just miss a lot of hard work, that's all!

I'll miss having to get up at midnight every night.

I'll just miss the aggravation.

I'll miss the darkness and the noise.

All but two of these men had jobs of the lowest-paying types in the mines, and all of them were employed underground; in

TABLE 11

MEANINGS OF WORK WHICH WOULD BE MISSED
MOST UPON RETIREMENT

Meanings of Work	No.	Per Cent
The income	85	51
Nothing	10	6
Extra-economic considerations:		
Having something to do	29	41
Friends on the job	26	37
Satisfaction in doing a good job	13	18
Self-respect from the job	3	4
Total extra-economic consideration	71	43
Total	166	100

other respects they seemed to follow no pattern. A major factor in their response evidently was their low job grade; but this is not a sufficient explanation, for their views were not shared by others of similar position. It will be correctly supposed that they were among the group who stated that their work had no meaning other than as a source of income.

The major extra-economic meaning of work which it was thought would be missed upon retirement was "having something to do," stated by 41 per cent of those naming such factors. It was shown in Table 9 that one of the meanings of work most favored by these men was the routine activity of the job, in which work becomes so much a part of living that it is difficult for the individual to imagine what his life might be without it. The comments which were made in connection with this reply leave little doubt as to its importance.

I would miss getting up and going to work.

I would miss going to work. It is a habit.

I want to keep busy and not stand around town moving from one shadow to another.

I would go crazy if I quit. I have to have something to do.

Hell, I almost go crazy around home now when I'm off for a day. I won't retire as long as I stay in good physical shape.

I don't want to stop working. I'm afraid I'd rot if I did.

I'd be miserable if I couldn't work.

I'd rather wear out than rust out. I probably wouldn't like sitting around. All I'd be doing would be waiting for the undertaker to come and get me.

The emotional background of many of these statements is quite apparent.[27] It is considerably easier to recognize this than to understand it. When an individual states that his work gives him "something to do," does he refer solely to its routine character as an activity which absorbs time and attention? If so, then any activity whatsoever, whether productive or not, might serve as well; but it would hardly be expected that so much concern would be evidenced in discussing the possibility of retiring. The strength of feeling becomes understandable if the statement is considered to be symbolic of other, more specific meanings which the individual cannot or does not wish to express. The belief that one is a useful member of society so long as he continues to work; the stimulation of purposeful, co-ordinate activities with others; the postponement of a reckoning with the significance of one's life—all these and other vaguely perceived ideas are perhaps involved. In the absence of concrete data bearing upon the problem, it is useless to speculate further. But certainly the mere statement that one continues to work because he needs something to do tells nothing of the nature of the personality structure of which the need is an expression. The problem can

27. It was noted in the interviews that the men who answered in this manner were more than usually apprehensive regarding the nature and purpose of the interview. Questions as to how the man's name had been obtained and whether the interviewer had been sent by the company usually came from this group.

only be stated here; more penetrating inquiries than those of this study would be required to understand what it involves.

The second largest proportion of the group, 37 per cent of those who named an extra-economic factor, said that they mainly would miss their friends on the job when they retired. The belief was stated in several ways:

I'll miss my working buddies more than anything.

I'm with a bunch of men who have worked together for thirty years. We have a good time. I've never missed a shift.

The mines are kind of a family affair. I'll miss that.

I missed my wife when she died; I guess I'll miss my friends when I retire.

I'll miss joking with the fellows going back and forth to work.

Essentially, these statements express the same kind of feeling; however, the methods by which it is conveyed are of three types. There is, first, reference to the long period of work with the same group, implying the emergence of friendships and personal attachments which are not actually described; second, reference to family and marital relationships, that is, an effort to imagine the nature of the experience of retirement in terms of these relationships and simultaneously an indication of their nature; and, third, reference to the quality of the interaction, namely, as a joking relationship.[28] It is clear that something more than a matter-of-fact attitude based upon the decency, honesty, or skill of fellow-workers is involved. The quality of the sentiment is of a depth and complexity produced only by long years of intimate association.

When it is recalled that these men had worked as miners an average of forty years, it is not surprising to learn that they believed they would miss their friends when they retired. It might

28. Each of these three modes of expression was encountered repeatedly. The first is perhaps the most obvious and most frequent reply to a question of this type; it is not for this reason necessarily the most superficial, however. The second is particularly interesting as an effort to convey understanding by analogy to the most intimate type of relationship. The third, referring to joking, was quite frequently used, often with illustration; it represents a formalization of the behavior of those whose activities are necessarily and continuously interrelated.

be expected that friendships would be mentioned more frequently. However, in the small communities in which most of the men live, they often see their fellow-workers in the course of ordinary activities—at church, lodge, tavern, movies, shopping, etc. Unlike workers in a metropolitan factory, the place of work is not the major or exclusive situation in which fellow-workers are met. Moreover, it is nearly always possible for a retired miner to locate an old friend of his own age level, often within the immediate neighborhood.[29] Thus retirement does not necessarily signify loss of contacts with friends. These facts must have been in the minds of many men as they answered the interviewer's question. It is not possible to estimate how much larger the proportion who named friendship as the factor which they expected to miss might have been if account could have been taken of this unspoken assumption. Here, as at other points, the response to an inquiry depended in some measure upon the nature of the communities in which the men lived.

Less than one-fifth of the men stated that they would miss the sense of satisfaction which comes from doing a good job. There are few jobs in the mines which involve craftsmanship in any traditional sense. The work is specialized; the individual as an individual creates nothing. Men of the same job grade receive the same pay, and for the older man there is little incentive to do a better job than the next fellow.

Only 4 per cent stated that they would miss the self-respect which came from their jobs. The proportion is significant by reason of its smallness, for it indicates that few men believe their work has enhanced their self-respect or that self-respect will be lessened by leaving their jobs. It was noted in a previous section that the kind of pride in the job which these men felt was distinctively individualistic rather than reflective of the opinion of the community or society. In any subsequent inquiry of this nature it would be desirable to raise the question whether the self-respect of the individual is not actually enhanced by retirement from his occupation.

29. Small groups of retired miners gathered on the downtown street corners on sunny afternoons are a familiar sight in nearly all communities in the area.

Attitude toward Retirement and the Meaning of Work

It is appropriate at this point to turn attention more specifically to the problem of the relationship between the several meanings of work which have been discussed and the wish to retire at a certain age. The subjects had been asked whether they would prefer to retire or to continue working upon reaching age 65.[30] The replies were cross-classified according to the statements described previously regarding the features of their jobs which the men thought they would miss most when they retired, as shown in Table 11.[31] Of those who had stated that they would miss the income from working, 51 men, or 63 per cent, stated that they would prefer to stop working, and 37 per cent to continue. In comparison, only 36 men, or 51 per cent, of those who had stressed various intrinsic meanings of work wished to stop working, and 49 per cent to continue. Thus the proportion who believed they would miss various extra-economic meanings of their jobs and who wished to continue working was nearly one-third greater than the proportion who thought mainly of the income received.[32]

The hypothesis that those men whose work has assumed various extra-economic meanings are less desirous of retiring than those who think of their work primarily in terms of earning a living gains support from these data. The percentages cited above would be changed if the prevailing wage scales were altered or if the amount or conditions of eligibility for the miners' pension were changed. Nevertheless, at the time of this study, the balance of factors was weighted in the direction of retirement for those whose job interest was primarily economic. To the extent that the work of some men had become mean-

30. The data presented in these paragraphs may be compared with that of Tables 9 and 11. Age 65, used as the basic age for this inquiry, was in advance of the actual age of all but 10 per cent of the group and thus represented a possible future date for retirement. It also represented the age at which the men would be eligible to receive both the miners' pension and Social Security payments.

31. The ten men who had stated that they would miss nothing about their jobs upon retiring were not included in the present analysis.

32. A difference in percentages of this magnitude might be expected to occur by chance in 9 out of 100 random samples drawn from the same universe.

ingful in its own right, they tended to desire to remain at work beyond the age which has come to be looked upon as the customary age for retirement.

This analysis may be carried further through an examination of the differences in proportions of men wishing to retire or to continue working who had subscribed to each of the several meanings of work. The data pertaining to the meanings of work which were presented in Table 11 are subclassified, in Table 12, according to stated preference for retirement or continued work.

TABLE 12

MEANINGS OF WORK ACCORDING TO WISH TO RETIRE
OR TO CONTINUE WORKING AT AGE 65

MEANINGS OF WORK	PREFERRED STATUS AT AGE 65	
	Stop Working	Continue Working
Having something to do............	12	17
Friends on the job.................	17	8
Satisfaction in doing a good job......	5	8
Self-respect from the job............	2	1
Total........................	36	34

Although the numbers in this table are too small to permit definite conclusions, one may discuss the trends. Those who would miss the "satisfaction in doing a good job" or "having something to do" tend to desire to continue working. Presumably, they see little or no possibility of making up by leisure activities for the losses they will suffer from retirement.

On the other hand, less than one-third of the men who stated that their work was meaningful because of the opportunities for associating with friends on the job wished to continue working after age 65. This is the smallest proportion in any of the four categories. The fact seems to corroborate the statement that the expectation which the men have of the continuation of friendships in the community following retirement reduces the importance of friendship as a factor in the desire to remain at work. The men who replied in this manner were also distinguishable in terms of related characteristics: they had the longest average history of work as miners; a larger than average proportion were lifetime residents of the communities in which they lived; they had on the average considerably less education than either of the two preceding groups; a larger proportion than of any other group were the sons of farmers; a greater than average proportion believed that a man should retire "when his health suffers"; and they included a smaller proportion than any other group of men whose chief concern regarding retirement was "to continue to be a part of the world" or "to be of use to others." Several of these traits seem to be inter-related in their bearing upon willingness to retire: long years of work, low wages, farm background, and lack of concern with the idea of "usefulness." Again, personal and occupational history seems to be functionally important in relation to feelings regarding retirement.

In summary, it appears that the hypothesis of this discussion regarding the relationship between meanings of work and willingness to retire has, in general, been supported by the analysis of somewhat limited data. Among the men of this group, a considerable majority of those to whom work has meant mainly a source of income desire to retire at age 65; in contrast, a majority of those who have found other meanings in their work wish to continue working. Two meanings of work seem to have the greatest degree of relationship to the desire to continue: satisfaction in doing a good job and having something to do. The number of men stating the former meaning is small and has received only occasional attention in the preceding pages; the men who stated the latter meaning, however, have figured prominently throughout this discussion. From the standpoint of retirement policy, no one of the groups can be said to be more deserving of attention than another. In terms of the magnitude of the problem which they are likely to present to both the mining companies and the union, the greater problem will be produced by the latter group of men, whose routine work activity has apparently become so fundamental to their whole pattern of life.

After Retirement

The desire to retire or to continue working beyond retirement age depends partly upon the individual's conception of what his life would be like after retirement. Personal observations and discussions of retired fellow-workers had made most of the men of this group apprehensive concerning the problems which they might encounter following retirement. Very few of them pictured the path ahead as free from difficulties.

In an effort to learn what these difficulties were thought to be, the men were asked what their major worries were regarding retirement. The pattern of responses was similar to that resulting from some of the questions previously discussed: they were worried about maintenance of income and standard of living, having something to do, condition of health, etc.[33] Little purpose would be served here by a detailed description of these responses; it will be more profitable to consider them in relation to the broader context of the interview discussion in which they were given. Four general conclusions seem justified: (1) nearly all the men were seriously concerned with the problems which they believed retirement would bring; (2) their worries pertained to several possible problems rather than one; (3) the most frequently expressed concern, regarding income and standard of living, often seemed to be a stereotyped rationalization of fundamental anxieties of a different character; and (4) few men had formulated what could be judged to be realistic plans for meeting the problems which they expected to encounter. The third and fourth points are the topics of the following discussion.

The predominant concern with economic problems in retirement undoubtedly arises partly from a lack of financial reserves and the apparent inadequacy of the miners' pension. Yet it would be unwarranted to accept at face value the statements of all men who said they were chiefly concerned with

33. The distribution of responses was as follows: keeping up standard of living, 41 per cent; keeping busy, 25 per cent; being able to care for self, 15 per cent; being of use to others, 5 per cent; being part of activities of others, 4 per cent; no worries about retirement, 9 per cent.

these problems. When asked what they would miss about their jobs when they retired or what worried them about retirement, they responded in terms which they believed would be understandable and acceptable to the questioner: they said that they "needed the income" or "had to have a job to keep up with expenses." Thus the initial replies to these questions centered about economic factors. However, in the subsequent discussions it frequently became evident that the underlying apprehensions had to do more with feelings that retirement meant uselessness or lack of recognized social function than with economic problems. The fears were of retirement as a threat to the organized personality, with its involvements in and dependence upon work-related activities, rather than of loss of income or living standards.[34] Unwilling or unable to verbalize these feelings in other than conventional ways, the replies assumed the form which has been described. It is probable that some considerable proportion of those who stated that their main worries about retirement had to do with economic matters should be added to those who described their concern with problems of status, usefulness, and social participation in a less equivocal manner.

The extent of the interest in problems of retirement was clearly demonstrated in the discussions of retirement plans. Fifty-four per cent of the men had passed the pension age of 60 or would reach it within a year. Of these, a few said they had made no retirement plans; 70 per cent, however, expected to continue in some economically productive activity, while 26 per cent planned only to "rest" and "enjoy life."

The thinking of those who hoped to work after retirement is illustrated in these statements:

Every man should prepare for his retirement. He should go into farming or some other useful thing, because if he remains inactive for any length of time his life is as good as over. My father went back to farming after he left the mines, and that's what I plan to do.

Just because I retire when the time comes, I'm not going to just sit around and watch the world go by. I am going to start a truck farm, or raise chickens, or something like that; but I won't just be idle.

34. This is illustrated by the quotations in the section immediately preceding.

I was thinking that after I quit at the mine maybe I would go down to one of these plants and try to get on. I might be able to get on as a guard. It would be a good job, guard duty; wouldn't take too much out of a man.

I want to go into some kind of mechanical work like I am doing now. That would be the only reason I would quit at the mines, if I could get a job like that. I might as well be dead if I couldn't work.

These plans appear reasonable enough at first glance, especially those of men who plan to farm, for many of them came from farm backgrounds and have continued to do part-time farming while working in the mines. However, the ambition to "get a little piece of ground" is not confined to these men; others, who have neither capital nor experience, share the same intention, and for them such plans can only be judged to be unrealistic. As to those who hope to find employment of some other type following retirement, the probability is that they will spend weeks, perhaps months, in unsuccessful job-seeking, with the gradually growing realization that they are retired in fact if not in spirit. A limited number of interviews with men who had retired earlier indicated that very few of those who sought work had found it. In a broader sense, the most significant feature of the above statements is the intensity of the feeling that a man must continue to work after retirement.

One-fourth of the men of retired age said they had made no specific plans.

When I retire, I'm not goin' to do nairy a thing but rest.

I sure do look forward to retiring. I'm going to sleep late and just enjoy life.

I'm just goin' huntin' and fishin' when I retire.

In comparison with the previous group, these men intend to retire in something more than an official sense. How long they will be satisfied to "rest" before they begin to fidget is problematic; they may soon join the ranks of the gardeners and job-seekers. Nevertheless, they have no initial resistance to the prospect of retirement; they seem able to accept the fact that their life's work is nearly over without feeling that life itself is ending. Whether they will be better adjusted than those who have made positive plans cannot be judged.

A final comment is appropriate concerning these retirement plans as they relate to company and union policy. With the exception of the last group, all the men approach retirement fearfully. Their plans are concentrated largely upon the objective of finding something to do to take the place of their jobs. Their insecurity is symbolized mainly in economic terms, but it is more subtle and complex than this. Both companies and union could lessen the problems of adjustment to retirement by instituting routine discussions with each man well in advance of his retirement. Such discussions could aid in developing more effective plans than most men seem to have evolved for themselves. They might also deal with the problems of health, recreation, community participation, friendship, and family life, which are as important as finances, not only after a man leaves his work, but in the last several working years as well.

IV

The Retail Salespersons: Men and Women

Selling, viewed as a way of earning a living, is beset by a number of popular stereotypes. On the one hand, the high-pressure, foot-in-the-door salesman has fostered the idea that salesmen are a special, sometimes obnoxious, breed of human being; while, on the other hand, the fact that people can make a living at selling without special training or apprenticeship fosters the idea that "anybody can get behind a counter and sell." Either view suggests that selling is something one turns to when one cannot do or find anything else. This, of course, is an injustice to the great majority of people engaged in direct selling, whether they are "on the road" for the wholesale houses, "on the floor" for the retail stores, behind the counter in a grocery, or calling on people in their homes. Considering such a variety of means, merchandise, and clientele, we would expect that sales work would have many meanings to the people engaged in it and that some would not wish to leave it for retirement or any other reason.

But what do salespeople have to say about this? The present investigation into the meaning of work to members of various occupational groups affords an opportunity for one group to speak for itself. This chapter will deal with the meaning of work to men and women who sell in a large metropolitan department store. It will deal also with their attitude toward retirement and the relationship between attitudes toward retirement and the meaning of work.

Two reasons, in addition to intrinsic interest, prompted the selection of this group for inclusion in the present study: (1) it represents the so-called "white-collar class," thus permitting some comparison between white-collar workers, tradesmen, and professional people, and (2) both men and women are employed on similar jobs, thus permitting comparisons between the sexes, an opportunity which is not afforded to the same degree by the trades and professions.

Taking together all the occupations reviewed in this book, it is expected that recognition of meanings of work, beyond earning a living, will increase in each group as the skill level of the occupation rises and that persons who recognize meanings in work other than earning a living will prefer to work past the age of 65. Since salesmanship requires both social and intellectual skills, we would expect salespeople as a group (1) to stress some meanings of work other than earning a living and (2) to prefer to work beyond the age of 65.

However, when sex is taken as a variable, we must consider other factors, such as the fact that in our culture men are expected to have a vocation or a career, while women are expected to be primarily homemakers. Though these expectations are not nearly so rigid with regard to women as formerly, the women of the present study are all members of a generation which shared those expectations for the greater part of their lives. On the basis of this difference, then, it might well be (1) that women would not find as many meanings in work or stress them as highly as men and (2) that as a group they would be more willing or eager to retire than men.

It has been suggested that the type of adjustment in retirement is dependent on the individual's ability to find satisfactions to compensate for the loss of those formerly found in work. This assumes that the needs and expectations of every individual are rooted in his fundamental character structure and are not likely to alter abruptly with a sudden change of life-situation. Thus we would expect that every individual would seek his particular kinds of satisfaction in any situation he might find himself and that his attitude toward any change would be shaped by his expectations of fulfilling his needs and desires in the new situation. If this is the case, those who find a great variety of meanings in work and who stress them highly may have difficulty in finding the variety and challenge they desire in the more limited opportunities afforded in retirement and consequently would not wish to retire. On the other hand, those workers who recognize fewer meanings and care about them less strongly may encounter less difficulty (and possibly greater satisfaction) in the limited opportunities and demands of retirement and consequently would wish to retire. Similar reasoning lies behind the expectation that men, having no role in society to replace that of working man, would prefer to continue working; while women, having a role valued by society to step into, would wish or be willing to retire.

THE COMPANY

The study was carried out in a large metropolitan department store with a well-established reputation for reliability and good customer relationships. Its personnel policies are liberal. Employees are encouraged to discuss problems with personnel representatives, and transfers to more congenial departments or to another kind of work are facilitated if requested. With regard to the sales force, training policies emphasize the importance of friendliness and service to the customer—making the store a pleasant place to shop so that people will want to come back.

The method of computing salaries for salespeople varies with the type of sales section. In sections where sales are seasonal, or where the selling prices of articles are too small to allow a high commission rate, salespeople are paid a fixed salary, plus 1 or 2 per cent "incentive commission" on all sales. In other sections the salesperson is paid from 3 to 8 per cent "straight commission" on all sales, with no guaranteed salary. They are assured a minimum weekly "draw," but, if they fail to earn that much, they must make up the amount by deductions from subsequent earnings. A few people who have responsibilities in addition to selling are on a straight salary basis, with no commissions.

The company does not have a compulsory retirement age. Its policy regarding retirement is to retain the individual as long as he is carrying out his job satisfactorily, unless he fails to pass a physical examination given by the company's physician. Once the employee reaches 64 years of age, these examinations are compulsory annually. Some older salespersons who may pass the physical examination and also maintain a sufficiently high sales record may nevertheless be released because of poor customer relationships. Several interviewees, for instance, referred to people they had known who were "let go because they had become snappy with the customers." Workers who wish to retire at 65 after fifteen years or more of service receive a pension from the company. The amounts are determined by fixed formula and may be taken in monthly payments or as a lump sum.

In addition to its flexible view toward age and retirement, the company has a liberal policy toward age and hiring. The average age of its employees is higher than that of any other department store in Chicago. A number of interviewees with less than a year or only a few years of service remarked that no other place would hire them because of their age. Moreover, a number of retirees from stores with a fixed retirement age have moved to the company where the study was conducted and continued to sell, sometimes bringing with them their own established clienteles.

HOW THE STUDY WAS CARRIED OUT

Thirty-seven salesmen and an equal number of saleswomen, all between the ages of 55 and 70 years, participated in the study. All were American-born except eight men and four women who came to this country from the British Isles in their youth or early adulthood. The median wage for men was $90 per week; and that for women, $55 per week. Length of service ranged from a few months to 40 years, the average being 16 years for the men, and 12 years for the women.

The interviews were held in a private office during slack hours (early morning and late afternoon) of the summer. Personnel representatives of the company arranged them and explained their purpose, stressing that the proceedings would not be known to company officials and that participation in the study was requested but not required. The average length of the interviews was about one hour. The questions asked in the interviews were:

Tell me about your job. What do you like most about it? What do you dislike? What would you miss most about your job if you weren't working? How did you get started in selling? Did you have any long-range plans when you first started to work? How do you feel about those plans now? If, twenty-five years ago, you had had enough money to do anything you wanted, what do you think you might have done? What would you do now? Do you have any plans regarding retirement? How do you feel about the idea? What would you miss most about work if you were to retire?

The fact that interviews were conducted on company premises, on company time, and through company co-operation must be recognized as having some effect on the nature of the statements made by the interviewees. However, generally good relations between company and employees maximize the possibility that interviewees could accept the situation as explained to them and would feel that they could express themselves freely. Rapport was generally good, and most interviewees talked freely and at length, often without prompting from the interviewer. It must be remembered, however, that the study group is a special one because it includes only older workers from one particular store.

ANALYZING THE INTERVIEWS

The following meanings of work were recognized and used in analyzing the content of the interviews:

2. Activity
    a) Mental (something to think about)
    b) Physical (something to do)
    c) Daily routine
3*a*. Self-respect
3*b*. Recognition or respect of others
4. Association
    a) With co-workers
    b) With customers
5*a*. Purposeful activity
    (1) Problem-solving or task fulfilment
    (2) Superior accomplishment
5*b*. Creativity and intrinsic enjoyment
5*d*. Service to others

Whenever an interviewee spoke of any of these meanings, an estimate was also made of the degree of importance—slight, moderate, or great—which this meaning had for him. Finally, each interviewee was given a "value-of-work score" derived by totaling weighted values (slight, 1; moderate, 2; great, 3) of recognized meanings.

No estimate was made of the value of earning a living as a meaning of work, because it was held to be a constant often taken for granted by the interviewees. The emphasis in this chapter is on the presence or absence of other meanings and their usefulness as possible predictive criteria for attitudes toward and adjustment to retirement.

A second person rated twenty cases to test the reliability of the scoring method for these interviews. Agreement between the reviewer and the author was 83 per cent[1] with regard to the identification of meanings recognized by each individual and 73 per cent[2] with regard to the estimate of the degree of importance the recognized meaning had for the individual.

"THE SELLING GAME"

Retail sales work is different from other occupations in its wide range of skills and money return. The salesperson in a department store may be handling small items which require little or no personal involvement beyond the act of putting an article into a box or bag and ringing up the sale, or he may be a person whose personality, knowledge of the merchandise, and skill in presenting it are major factors in the completion of every sale. For the less skilled salesperson in the less demanding sales sections, pay may be at the minimum rate of 90 cents per hour, while for the skilful salesman in the most remunerative sales sections it may run as high as $5.00 per hour. Furthermore, there are those who turn to selling because it is the only thing they can do (other than service or labor jobs), and there are others who have attended to and mastered all the art of salesmanship because it seems to them to provide the greatest challenge and outlet for their capacities.

For instance, one who earned the minimum weekly salary said:

1. There were twenty cases, with seven possible categories, making a total of 140 possible codings. The two reviewers agreed in 116 of these.

2. In each of the 140 possible codings, the reviewers were scored from 0 (no agreement) to 3 (perfect agreement) points. Perfect agreement throughout would result in a total agreement score of 420 points. The two reviewers had a score of 326 points.

Mrs. B.: I do think there's more money upstairs. Hardly worth while down in the basement any more. There's no commission. I think it would be very interesting to get at least 1 per cent. We're supposed to get commission—but I got commission twice last year, and that was all.

Q. Oh? Well, how did that happen?

A. Well, we have a certain quota to make every day, and there's lots of days you don't make that quota, you fall back into what they call the "red," and right now I'm in the red for $65 or $75, so I can't collect commission till I make that.

Another woman who sold small articles at a counter was among those who did not wish to work. She preferred music and painting and charitable activities on her own time to selling for someone else. A portion of her interview follows:

Q. What do you like best about selling?

A. Just seeing people. Talking to people.

Q. Would you miss that if you couldn't work here?

A. I don't think so. I'd have other things to do and think about. If I could afford it, I would. I'd find other interests. I know that. Above all, I would help other people, lonely people. Like I have been.

Q. Do you prefer selling one thing more than another—of the various items you have sold?

A. No, I don't think so. It's all selling.

Q. Is a small store different from a big department store?

A. It's just about the same wherever you go.

Q. When you're away from the job, do you miss it?

A. Yes, I do.

Q. What do you miss?

A. Oh, probably the idea, the routine, or something. I couldn't quite explain.

In contrast, the highest-paid woman in the group, who had worked during her married life and who wished to continue working, said:

Mrs. H.: I should have been a singer, or I should have been an actress. I have always had acting ability, and that aptitude is my selling power. There is no question about it, selling is acting. You have to act to sell, and *I mean act!* You have to feel entirely and completely in sympathy with the mood of the customer. You have completely to subject yourself to the feelings of the customer.

Now the other day a gentleman came in and came to me to buy a particular thing. I suggested something else instead for reasons which were obvious in view of what he told me was the purpose he wished to achieve.

He said, "Don't start giving me that!" So I sat down beside him and let him talk. He talked and he talked, and he considered this and that, and he argued himself all the way out of the idea, and then he said, an hour later, "You know—what did you say first?" And he repeated the suggestion that I had made at the very first, and that is what he settled for. And I made the sale simply by the way I handled it in letting him talk.

Q. Would you miss work if for some reason you weren't working?

A. Yes—yes.

Q. What would you miss most?

A. I think, to be perfectly truthful about it, the thing I miss most is being able to project myself into a sphere, conquer it, and retire with a pleased feeling because I have conquered it.

Q. How would you advise anyone who was thinking of starting out on selling as a career?

A. I would tell anyone starting out in the selling game to take it up as a profession, not as just some little happenstance thing.

"If You Work a Little Harder, You Can Make Yourself More Money"

Close approximation of money reward to performance on the job is more apparent in sales work than in other white-collar occupations, as one of the men from the men's clothing department pointed out:

Selling, I think, is the most independent deal that there is. I think that. You more or less have control of your earnings; you have control of your hours. It's entirely up to the man himself. If you sell, work a little harder, promote, you can make yourself more money. Or if you want to take it a little easier . . . but as long as you produce, you might produce a little less than the other fellow, but you're not going to be out on the street. You always get paid for it. In selling I've always wanted to work on commission, because if you get a straight salary and you don't make it, you're either going to get fired, or you're going to get your salary cut. But if you're working on a straight salary and you make *over* that, you have to squeeze nearly any employer to get an extra five dollars or ten dollars a week out of them. He may give you five and two years later he may give you another five, but if you're working on a commission you always get what you earn.

Commission rates, however, do not always reward the attentive salesperson, especially if he is selling lower-paying merchandise, as one of the men who sold shirts and pajamas in the basement pointed out:

Of course, the idea of selling, especially in this line of business, is to get rid of one customer as soon as you can so you can take care of another one. . . . You have people waiting. You can spend a lot of time talking with someone who just buys one little item, and in the meantime you lose a lot of other people, a lot of sales. People don't want to wait, and you've got to take care of them.

This quotation illustrates one of the dilemmas of the successful salesman. He can hardly succeed in selling unless he enjoys dealing with people, and yet this liking cannot stand as an end in itself but becomes a means toward an end—the completion of a sale. Although there are many who enjoy the personal aspect of their work because good personal relationships have intrinsic value for them, no salesperson fails to appreciate the direct value of such good relationships to his own purse. To a great extent he finds that he must distribute his favors discriminately or he is no salesman.

However, the attitude prevails among many that the satisfactions they derive from selling, whatever they may be, are more important than the money gained from selling fast. One man chose to leave the store because, as he said,

the store is turning more to the promotional side, to volume merchandising, instead of quality merchandising. They might take issue with me on that, but the two of them do not combine, especially in the sense. . . . I don't know too much about the other departments . . . but in the clothing department—if you've got a department that's very, very busy and rushed, and you have to make twice as many sales to make the amount of dollar volume, you cannot give customers the service—I don't care how good you are or how good your store is. You cannot give them the attention to details which the finer trade . . . not necessarily finer trade, but the higher-priced trade, requires.

This attitude is not only found among those who deal with and wish to continue to deal with higher-priced merchandise. It is also expressed by others, such as this woman who sold housewares:

I like to be able to talk about merchandise. I don't like it when people say, "Here!" (*Demonstrates somebody handing a package and reaching for money.*) I like to tell about this, what it's made of, what the use of it is, whether it will be durable. I like to talk about it. I don't like this over-the-counter handing of merchandise and taking the money. To me that isn't selling. . . .

Now we have people down there in the section that take in lots more money than I do. I know they do. I've watched them, and I've listened to them how they sell. They'll take a thing like this (*reaches toward an in-out correspondence box on the desk*) and say, "Isn't that beautiful!" Why I wouldn't say it was beautiful. It isn't beautiful. My first thought would be that it was *useful*, because there's nothing beautiful about it. It may be useful, and it may not, but it isn't beautiful. Not in my mind. I have one person in particular in mind. About the only thing she ever says is, "Isn't it beautiful!" She'll take a pan lid and say, "Isn't it beautiful!" It isn't beautiful. It either fits or it doesn't fit . . . but she makes a sale, so maybe I'm all wrong.

I had a man who wanted a towel-holder—a towel-holder and paper-holder. Just before I came up I settled him. He's going to tile his bathroom sometime in the future, maybe in five years. He's going to have one kind of wall now, till he gets to the time when he can tile it, but if he gets something for what he has now, it's usually something that you attach to the wall with screws of some kind, but if he wants to use them later on he'll have to have the kind that are put on with cement. Now there was this possibility and that possibility. We settled every kind of problem. He wants to fill the bill for today and for five years from now. Now it was very interesting to work with him and try to solve his problem. It was less than ten dollars, but it was a very satisfying case because the man was happy with what he got.

"They All Used To Call Me a Grabber"

In contrast to the value attached to good relationships with the customer and to the teamwork required in offices and industry, in any sales section where the salary is dependent on commissions the underlying spirit is necessarily one of competition between fellow-workers. While the dominant spirit expressed by the interviewees in the present study group was one of appreciation of fellow-workers (as will be shown later), two or three people spoke negatively of this aspect of work. One of these, a woman who had transferred to a nonselling job, gave the following as one of the reasons for the change:

There was quite a bit of jealousy, you know, amongst the girls. You'd make a sale—it wasn't them made it—or something like that. They all used to call me a grabber.

And a woman who is currently selling said, giving a little of both sides:

Working at selling you have something that you don't have in most jobs—you have more bickering in a way. I guess that's what you'd say— you have jealousy among the salespeople. If you have a good day and someone else just hasn't been getting the breaks at all—they say it that way. They resent it—maybe they think you're grabbing—sales-grabbing. You have a lot of resentment. But then if you have a bad day and some- one else is doing pretty well, they notice it, they sympathize with you. I think in general though there's a little more jealousy in that way than you find most places.

"The People Are Fascinating"

To these aspects of retail selling—its being open to many dif- ferent kinds of people with a wide range of skills and motivation, the competitive moment-to-moment pressure to make sales and the combination of material with social rewards for good personal relationships—to these must be added one further factor which distinguished retail selling from many other occupations, that is, the role of people in the salesman's work life. For most workers in nonsupervisory positions, the only people in their work life are their co-workers, and the relationship between them is for the most part purely an associative one. Here, on the other hand, "other people" are the salesman's object as well as his associates. They are his working material as much as is his merchandise; they are his challenge and his problem, his kaleidoscope of things to think about. Quotations throughout the remainder of the chapter will show the variety of ways in which people provide the sales- man's satisfactions and dissatisfactions in almost every phase of his work.

THE MEANING OF WORK

I think working is the greatest pleasure that mankind can ever think of. Without working he is lost to everything. He's lost the aspects of living. His money isn't going to do him much good for various reasons. All the old friends that he knew are dead, most of them. He has no particular place or any port of call. He is lonesome. He has to abide by his own force all the time, and that is bad for a man to be thinking of himself. Whereas, if he can keep on working, he will meet other people; it'll take his mind off himself completely. And he knows that he can earn some- thing.

This quotation emphasizes the variety and intensity of meaning that work can hold for an individual. Few were so well able to express themselves as was this salesman, but the following quotations will reveal the range and complexity of meanings recognized and valued by the participants in this study. The various categories are set forth in order of their importance to this group, a matter which will be discussed in detail in a later section.

Something To Do and Think About—Routine

"Something to do and think about," the meaning of work most often recognized as having value by the salespeople, revealed a difference between men and women as to which aspect—the "doing" or the "thinking"—was the more valuable. More than twice as many women as men said, "It takes your mind off things," or referred to selling as stimulating, varied, and educational. Following are several examples taken from women's interviews:

> You like to occupy your mind. In other words, I like to get out in the public. I like to hear things—what do you hear when you're home? You hear nothing. And as I said before, too much company is trouble. And I don't like that. I like to get out and hear something different.

> I like selling. I like people. Everybody's different. It isn't like an office job. It isn't the same. You have different people come in all the time . . . some nice . . . some not so nice . . . some likable . . . some you don't like. But it's always different and interesting.

Men also expressed similar feelings, though not so frequently. For example:

> They *should* work because it occupies their mind, and I think it improves everything. You've got to learn more—so many different people —they've got different ideas. You learn more. All that runs around in your brain and after you've heard what so many different people think, then you decide what you think. So many suggestions they give you.

Many women said, "Well, I wouldn't just want to stay home and go to bridge parties," or "scrub the floor three times a week when once would do," and "spend my time chasing dust." But many men were in a worse fix. They did not even have anything they would rather not do. Their idea of what they escape by working was more often like the following:

> Well, I have to think of my neighbors who are retired and have a nice home. I live out in ———, and I have a home and I know a lot of men around there that are 60–70 years old, and they don't have to work—

they have plenty of money. But if I had to sit around like they do and walk to the corner every afternoon and have a few drinks—and come back home and sit down—I would never do that. I've seen—I know quite a few men that do that. Have nothing to do—don't know what to do with yourself. I could not loaf around like some men. I never could. Sunday morning I get up at the same time—and I like to get to bed at a reasonable time, and I like to get up early. But I cannot—it never was in my nature to loaf around. I couldn't do it, and I wouldn't do it as long as I'm able to work.

I look at it this way. As long as I'm keeping my end up, not setting the world on fire, but keeping my end up and making money for the store and a little money for myself, that what's the use, why should I give up? What's the use? What would I do? You know, feeling in good health like I do, what would I do?

Association—Friendship

"Association," the meaning of work next most frequently mentioned as satisfying, has many facets. Some think of their customers as providing an opportunity for sociability and friendship:

And then you have so many friends among your customers. Like we started this sale yesterday. All day long it was "How are you, Mr. J.?" "Hello, Mr. J." People I knew, people I knew.

Well, I like to meet people—I think it's interesting to meet the different people. I've met a lot of them in twenty-five years of selling, and I've made a lot of very lovely friends through the contact of selling. While it's not something that has turned into social friendship, it's that even if they don't want anything they stop in to say, "Hello, how are you?" When I was in the hospital, I had several very nice cards and remembrances.

I'll tell you, office work was too much of a routine like—you know what I mean? The same thing all the time. It kind of got me down, you know. And I thought, well, I'd just get out. And, I tell you, this way I meet people more, and I like to meet people. I come from a large family, first of all. There were seven of us, and you know how it is when you have seven—we always had in those days. There wasn't so much—we had more parties at home—big ones—maybe you don't know, but that's how we had our parties in those days.

I like people. I like to meet them—it always means a lot in the morning when you greet them, you know.

I like selling because it gives you, oh, I don't know, you get acquainted with people and they're not customers, they're friends. And they think of me as though I were one of their family. That's the way I want to operate, and, if I can't operate that way, I don't want to operate at all.

Others find the customers a source of endless variety, a part of the continually changing scene:

It's meeting people—I like to handle people. I think meeting your different personalities every day—I think it's invigorating, and I just like it. Because you never meet the second personality alike, you know.

In an office you have only a certain kind of clientele. If you're in a law office, you have one kind; if you're in a business office, you just meet the people who work in that particular line of business. But in selling you contact people from the lowest to the highest. Some of them are almost illiterate—really, almost illiterate—and others are quite educated. Such a varied group.

I imagine it's mostly coming into contact with the people. I like to talk to people, meet strangers, see different types of people. You could write a book on selling, because every customer is handled differently.

"You have to be able to analyze people—size them up—they're interesting," say some, usually with the dual reference to enjoying the variety in personalities and recognizing the challenge of salesmanship involved:

My main theme would be people. What do I see in this individual, that personality—daily, what are my opportunities to read human nature, and reading it, meeting it, and overcoming it to my profit, and the profit of the store. That's a thrill.

Some get particular satisfaction from the groups with whom they have associated because of the "specialty" nature of their merchandise:

I like my little babies—up to teen-agers. I like them all, but the little ones, you can take their face in your hands and pet them. . . . There's something about the expression on a child's face. They love shoes better than anything else. You can get a child downtown for a new pair of shoes when you can't get them down for anything else. Not a hat, or a coat, or anything like a new pair of shoes. Their faces are wonderful!

And then I'm very much interested in the tall girls' problems. You know they have quite a hard time trying to get clothes and things like that.

Well—you—in selling furniture, you come in contact with customers that you possibly have to spend an hour, maybe two hours, making a sale, and you have a much more friendly attitude. They have, and we also have . . . you are meeting people who are setting up a house —young people—and they want to be directed right and everything else— you have—in fact, you make more friends. More friends.

But others have had particular dissatisfaction from special groups!

Q. Which do you prefer to sell?

A. Women's! I don't care to sell men's shoes!

Q. Why not?

A. I contend that one crabby man is worse than ten crabby women, and I don't think you get that many crabby women.

Q. Why is a crabby man worse than a crabby woman?

A. Just because they're worse than anything. I don't want to have anything to do with a crabby man.

Many people, both men and women, recognized the tie-in between good relations with customers and the completion of sales. The following expresses better than most the dual satisfaction entailed—real enjoyment together with awareness of its financial return:

I like people. I like to talk to people. I like to visit with them. I like to kid them. In other words, I'm a great kibitzer. As you can see, I'm rattling off here like I was wound up. So I enjoy selling people. In a store like this, you can sit down with a customer, you can talk to them, say, "Well, this is the first time I've ever sold you. Let's find out something about you first. How is your wardrobe? Do you have two suits, do you have four suits, do you have six suits?" And in the meantime as I go along I can bring out that "I have customers here who come in, I know what they wear, I know what they have, so when they come in they say, 'Well, give me a blue suit.' I say, 'Well, I know you don't want this plain one, you've got one like that, or you've got this.' So I go over and pick one out. It makes it so easy for you and easy for me." So the fellow gets thinking, "Well, this fellow must know something about his business."

Finally, expressions regarding relationships with their co-workers ranged from, "It's a nice bunch down there," to "They just opened their arms and took me in." When asked what they would miss most if they retired, many replied, "Well, I think your fellow-workers. I'd miss them a lot." One man with long service said:

> *Mr. Z.:* Working here's been nice—one of the nicest places I've worked. Know all the executives. They know me.
> *Q.* Well, how does that happen?
> *A.* Oh, well, waiting on them—one thing and another, you know.
> *Q.* What would you miss most if you retired?
> *A.* Well, I think the associates. So many people that you know—been here for a good many years, and that's what you miss. No, you can do a lot of things, but, after all, there's nothing like home, so to speak, and where you've been working all your lifetime, and most of the hours out of the twenty-four, you're there, that's what you miss . . . everybody's just a big family. It's like a big home, don't you know. People have died—used to be here, I knew very well.

And a woman who was afraid her health would soon force her to retire said:

> I'd miss most the girls. When you get used to the place, it means something, I think. Maybe if I had to give up the job, I would feel very, very lonesome. If I leave, I won't say anything to anybody but the boss because I'd shed tears.

This type of feeling predominated among these older salespeople, in spite of the competitive atmosphere mentioned earlier as a difficulty accompanying saleswork.

Purposeful Activity

Perhaps the most succinct statement of the kind of satisfaction that comes under the heading "purposeful activity" was the following made by one of the women previously quoted as the highest-paid individual in the whole group:

> I think, to be perfectly truthful about it, the thing I'd miss most is being able to project myself into a sphere, conquer it, and retire with a pleased feeling because I have conquered it. That is somewhat of an analysis of this thing, isn't it?

Both men and women frequently expressed a sense of satisfaction over the act of completing a sale, not because of the money, but more because of the sense of accomplishment of a task successfully carried through:

> It's meeting the people and accomplishing something. Doing something. It's sort of a challenge. I like it when I've had a good day. I

feel fine. I think it's a wonderful job. I feel as though I can do anything. When it's a bad day I think, "Isn't there anything else I can do? What a horrible way to earn a living!" But it isn't the money—I don't think of it so much in terms of money. It's the accomplishment—it's knowing that you have done the job, that you have made sales, that you have accomplished something that you set out to do.

[I like best] dealing with people and being able to put over a sale. Sometimes people aren't easy to sell, and, if you can use a little ingenuity in doing it, it gives you a sort of real satisfaction to have done them a service and to have done yourself a service at the same time. They're finding something they really want and should have, and it's you—your ingenuity that does it. I like to sell—I like to listen to the music of the cash register. Do I sound normal?

Some people like to know everything there is to know about their job:

And I always took an interest in everything. There are a lot of people in the store who don't seem to want to find out anything. Well, I was one of these people who made it my business to find out what it was, and also to know what goods were that sell, you see. I don't know, it's just my nature. Most of the other fellows in the department don't do that.

But as far as selling, it's just like eating a meal. I can just tell when I look at their feet what kind of shoes they're going to want. It comes so natural. They can't get anybody in there yet that's as fast. They'll have a hard time to beat me.

Finally, included in this general grouping are expressions of accomplishment in the past which retain importance in the person's eyes and give satisfaction in remembering:

I made progress in the selling—that's after selling better merchandise—and I thought after staying so many years in the basement I thought it was time to improve myself. I used to come upstairs with the customers from the basement, increased my commission by a great deal. Many times I'd capture two sales. They used to wonder how I did it, because those people that came to the basement, many times their spending money is limited. . . . I can handle a better trade.

Self-respect

While a feeling of self-respect could often be inferred from a salesman's emphasis on his accomplishments, the only expressions coded under this category were those which acknowledged a heightened feeling of personal worth as a result of working, or a statement that personal worth would be decreased if the person were not working. The first of these was most often expressed as satisfaction over the ability of the person to take care of himself:

My family will never let me down. Still I would never want them to care for me. You might know that I'm just that independent. I would be worse than dead if I had to come to them and say, "Well, I can't work any more, you'll have to take care of me. Or *will* you take care of me!" And I'm trying to save myself all that heartache.

You need it to keep feeling like a responsible person. You want to be independent. . . . I just have the feeling that if I let things get away from me, if I once drop out, I won't get back in again. I want to hold on to the reins as long as I'm able.

Others, like one who said, "I don't think we're put on earth just to sit," emphasize the loss of self-respect that would come from not working:

Oh, I'd want to be doing something. It—well, if you didn't work you'd be useless. You're meant to work. You should be producing—everybody should produce something. Just look around—take everything in nature. Look at the bees, for instance. They're always producing as long as they're alive. Animals—everything in nature keeps on, keeps on producing as long as it's alive. And we should too.

I come from a family that works. My father worked till he was 83 years old. I wouldn't just not work if I was a young man without any activity.

You have to use your mind and to use your ideas. You just have to keep useful in one way or another. An artist I would say would be working—or a writer. It's just as important as in the business world. You're just as important in your field, but you should be doing something.

Recognition from Others

For the salesperson recognition may come from his superiors, from his personal following, or from his family. Many of the accomplishments of his work life were reported in these interviews in terms of the recognition he received from others. Quite often the salesperson would refer to the value attached to his services by one of his superiors:

And I could hear what he said to her, while the phone was off the hook. I heard him say, "That's the best saleslady in the department."

Some, both men and women, spoke at great length of past or present accomplishments which had brought them recognition:

When I got back from my vacation, I went over to the ——— Avenue Store. The manager over there didn't like the idea of me coming in. And he sort of tried to work against me, in every way possible. Well, what happened? This is sort of a fairy tale, and I don't think everybody would believe me, but I have letters and wires at home now that would bear me out on what I'm saying. It may not seem probable, but from the first day that store started to do business. Ordinarily it did about two hundred dollars worth of business. From two hundred it went to three hundred, then to four hundred, then to a thousand. Mr. ——— sent me wires of congratulations. "What on earth are you doing with that store," he wired.

Well, I wasn't doing anything. It wasn't any changes I made. I didn't do a thing. What happened—they saw the way I worked, and they started working the way I did. Before they thought every customer was a three- or four-hundred dollar order. But he wasn't. You know, not everybody is, and they never will be. But the way you build up a trade you treat every customer the same, whether he buys or doesn't buy. You know you get the office girl who comes down from one of the buildings on the avenue. You get the person that's just shopping, but maybe they change from shopper to customer. You treat them right— and you can't get a bell-ringer[3] if you don't know how to talk to them.

Mr. ———, who was general manager, he came down. "A.," he said, "have you gone crazy?"

"What do you mean," I said. "I'm not doing anything. It isn't me. It's all the fellows. They're making the sales, I'm not."

Well, that store went for over two thousand dollars a day. And everybody was asking, "What has this guy A. got that everybody just loves him." I said, "Ask Miss Wilson, she'll tell you."

"Miss Wilson," he said, "what do you make of this. What's this guy doing. Do you know why everybody loves A.?"

"Do you know what Mr. A. is?" she asked him. "He's a human being." That's exactly what she said, "He's a human being, and he treats all the customers as though they were human beings, and they love him

3. "Bell-ringers" are steady customers who like to have the salesperson telephone them from time to time to tell them what is available and inquire as to their needs. This usually means a sizable order if the "bell-ringer" is ready to buy, and a number of salesmen said that their list of telephone numbers helped them over slack periods.

for it." Well, I said as long as I live and as long as I have anything to say, they'll always love me.

Signs of esteem from their customers are also valued:

We had a courtesy day—courtesy award. I had seven awards. There were three or four people had one, and one had three—so you see I'm not the type of girl who just comes in to pass the time and collect the salary.

You're not selling them merchandise; you're selling them you. You're selling them the confidence in you. The confidence that you know your merchandise. That you know what you're talking about. That if you say, "That's the suit for you to take," he'll feel, "Well, that's right." . . . Well, the people who come in to me, or rather that come to a man that knows his business, feel the same way about it.

Some women felt keenly the approval they received from family members for work they had done and were doing:

My husband gives me all the credit in the world for being where we are today. You know we could have been way down.

Creativity or Intrinsic Enjoyment

No one recognized any area of creativity in selling other than brief references to displaying one's merchandise attractively or giving suggestions for color schemes in selling draperies or materials for clothing. However, among salespeople enjoyment is often derived from the merchandise itself:

Some women go more for this fol-de-rol stuff where I don't. Silver to me—well, it's a lasting investment, and, when you're selling sterling silver, you've got something to talk about—and you talk about it truthfully. It's something that turns into an heirloom—never wears out. It has sentimental value. It's real. It's solid. Of course I'm in the sterling end of it. Of course, I do sell plated wear too, but my stock is sterling stock.

Well, I love to sell oriental rugs—they have such beautiful designs. The colors are so beautiful. They're interesting—they're beautiful to see. It used to be that every one was different. There wasn't any of them alike. It was like looking at a painting.

Some like the associations inherent in the merchandise, such as liking draperies because one is interested in people's homes:

It's a very interesting department, and I like to talk to customers about their homes. They're doing things, and you get to help them. They're doing things for their rooms. And just talking to people in this particular line of work, you do that all the time. And there's lots of color in it. I like to work with different types. You have to help people plan their windows. You're talking about rugs and the things they have in their homes.

Some women like to sell clothing because they are interested in fashion and clothes:

I don't know—it's just interesting I guess—seeing people in new clothes, you know, and everything like that—seeing them satisfied—happy about it. I think everybody likes to buy new things.

When the new things come in, in the spring and in the fall, there's sort of a thrill about new styles and new fabrics and all that sort of thing I like.

Service to Others

Though many persons in the present study recognized that selling means serving the customer, relatively few mentioned this as one of the valued aspects of their work. Those who did revealed a feeling of personal satisfaction in helping the customer find what he wanted:

Pleasing my customer—I mean so that she's just really happy—that's the thing I like best—that she's really happy. And I have customers who buy who really are happy. I have many customers who have really thanked me, not only once, but several times, for being patient and helpful. I think I would say being helpful is the most important thing. I enjoy selling when the customer goes away happy. That's what I like to aim for in selling.

There's a lot of satisfaction out of putting something on a man you know looks well on him, and that he's going to get a lot of compliments and he's going to be pleased and all that.

Well, it's the different people that you meet and the way in greeting them, coming in contact with them and helping them. Now a lot of people, they're undecided—they don't know what they want—and giving your assistance is a great help to them.

Service, as well as good personal relationships, has money value in addition to intrinsic value for salespeople:

I've always made it my business to fit shoes correctly. Now in my experience selling shoes I've found people that went into the shoe business that wanted to sell shoes more than fit shoes. Well, it's all right to sell a lot of shoes, too, but I always found it's best to sell your shoes critically. You build up a bigger clientele. I want to sell as much as I can. I want to sell those shoes so that they fit. I don't like this idea of selling shoes and having them come back.

Did Salespeople as a Group Stress Meanings of Work Other than Earning a Living?

The salespeople in the present study group recognized so many meanings in work that it was necessary, as noted above, to split several categories and to extend the list in order to cover their expressions in this regard. Table 13 presents the meanings of work reported by these men and women.

TABLE 13

FREQUENCY OF OCCURRENCE OF THE MEANINGS OF
WORK FOR SEVENTY-FOUR SALESPEOPLE—
MEN AND WOMEN
(In Per Cent)

Meaning of Work	Men	Women	Total
2. Something to do and think about.................	84	95	89
3, a. Self-respect...........	43	54	49
3, b. Respect of others......	49	41	45
4. Association.............	81	89	85
5, a. Purposeful activity	65	57	61
5, b. Intrinsic enjoyment....	32	62	47
5, d. Service to others......	35	46	41

The aspects of work most frequently mentioned as important to these people were "something to do and think about" and "association." Eighty-nine and 85 per cent of the total group, respectively, mentioned these meanings of work as having value for them.

Work was also highly valued for the opportunity it provided for "accomplishment"—a sense of satisfaction in meeting and solving a problem successfully. Sixty-one per cent of the total group expressed satisfactions of this kind. Between 45 and 50 per cent of the interviewees mentioned "self-respect," "the respect of others," and a special preference for their merchandise or pleasure in displaying it, which was coded as "intrinsic enjoyment." Forty-one per cent mentioned satisfaction derived from "service to others."

No one of these salespeople failed to recognize some meaning beyond earning a living, and almost 90 per cent recognized three or more meanings. Sixty-three per cent of the total group considered at least one meaning highly important and satisfying (two-fifths of these valued two or even three meanings very highly); 34 per cent were rated as considering at least one meaning as moderately important but no meaning highly important; and only 3 per cent were considered to derive only the lowest degrees of satisfaction from those meanings that were recognized.

These findings and the quotations presented in the preceding section indicate that salespeople, as expected, find meanings in their work beyond earning a living and that their work is, for the majority, a valued part of their lives.

Did the Women Value Work Less than the Men Did?

The saleswomen did not find fewer meanings in their work than men. There is some evidence that their awareness of the various aspects of work that were coded in this study was more extensive than the men's and that the men stressed the meanings that work had for them more strongly than the women. However, when these factors are combined into the value-of-work score, there is no evidence that the women in general valued their work either less or more than did the men.

One difference in the meaning of work to these salesmen as compared with the saleswomen appeared in the category "something to do and think about." "Something to do" and "something to think about" must be considered together because there is no way of knowing whether or not to infer mental as well as physical activity from such comments as, "You like to keep busy" or "You can't just sit with nothing to do." However, when a separate tally was made, for descriptive purposes, of those who said specifically, "It takes your mind off things," or who referred to selling as stimulating, varied, and educational, it was found that twice as many women as men expressed themselves in this way.

Thus the interview data do not bear out the expectation that women would value work less than men. It is likely that the high value women place on work is due to the fact that with the changing times—labor-saving devices, smaller dwellings, and smaller family units—the role of the woman in the home is often quite an empty one. The interview material itself bears this out, for many women said they would not want to go back to bridge parties and "chasing dust." Similarly, the emphasis on "something to think about" rather than "something to do" may be due to the fact that the women were acquainted, as the men were not, with the mental vacuum that accompanies routine work in a limited social setting and thus were more aware of the variety of interests "the outside world" had to offer.

RETIREMENT

Whatever the special circumstances of each case, and regardless of age, the feeling toward retirement of almost 65 per cent of the men could be summed up: "As long as I feel like I do now, I wouldn't want to quit. What would I do with my time?" The feeling toward retirement of almost 32 per cent of the women who did not want to retire could be summed up: "As long as I feel like I do now, I wouldn't want to quit, because I think you're more alive when you're working."

However, one would expect to find a variety of expressions in keeping with the general feeling and others in contrast to it. Following are some excerpts which, though limited, are representative of the range of attitudes expressed by the study participants.

Only slightly more than a third of the men and women expected to be financially able to retire. Among those salespeople who saw little possibility of having sufficient "to retire on" and who could hardly tell how they would feel if they had enough to live on comfortably were a salesman and a saleswoman, the latter a widow. They discussed the matter as follows:

Q. Do you have any plans for retiring?
Mr. P.: I couldn't. I haven't got any money. I could retire like anybody else if I had the money.
Q. Would you like to?
A. Oh, I don't know. I might. It'd all be in the circumstances. It would depend on how much money I had to do with.
Q. Well, if you had enough money to do anything you wanted, would you want to retire?

A. Oh, yes, naturally.

Q. What do you think you would do?

A. Do what I do every Sunday. Fool around—work around the house—travel a little.

Q. Do you think you would miss work?

A. I'm afraid I would. Yes, I think I would miss work.

Q. What would you miss about it?

A. Well, the associates mostly, I think. You know, when you're out in a place like this, you meet people all the time. Now, I've made wonderful friends, through customers. You see, we have a very nice place here. People come in, and they come back to you. You get to know them. And they send in their sons to you, and you work up a trade that way.

Q. Is there anything else you would miss about work if you weren't coming down?

A. No, outside of just the people I associate with—the people I eat lunch with every noon, and then I'm in the American Legion here, I'd probably drop out of that.

Mrs. W.: I never wanted to work when I didn't have to.

Q. How long do you expect to keep on working now?

A. Well, I have no other means of support so I guess I'll just have to keep working till I fall off my feet. (*Laughs.*) As I say, I have no other means of support, and I don't expect anybody to leave me any money—unless they raise Social Security to $200 a month.

Q. What would you do if you had all the money you needed to do anything you wanted to?

A. Well—just all the money? Well, I rather think it would be nice to travel. I'd like to have a—I've always enjoyed traveling in a car. I'm always taking trips with my sister. It's nice to travel, and, of course, it may seem that I'm too old maybe to take it up, but I used to play a lot of golf. Maybe if I had my strength back, maybe I couldn't. I don't know. I don't know just what hobby I would want to acquire. Maybe I'd get tired of it after a while.

Q. What do you think you would want to do if you got tired of that?

A. Oh, I might want to work a few days a week if I knew my life didn't depend on it.

Only a few of the men and women intend to retire at the age of 65 or before—two or three with considerable financial independence, the others with careful planning. For example, this 62-year-old man:

Q. What would be the main reason for your wanting to come back? If you had to quit?

A. Well—I like it here—you know—and I'd work out until I'm 65 at least—and keep occupied, you know. Of course, I'm counting on that little Social Security when it comes along to put a little sugar on my bread and butter—so. . . .

Q. But any time after 65 you don't plan to work on a regular basis?

A. Well, I hope not to. And I want to get around and see things and do things. I want to—I have been tied down all my life—so at 65, I ought to have a little joy and get around. You know how it is—I've always had to keep a home—and you have to keep your nose to the grindstone to do that.

On the other hand, about half of the men and one-third of the women who considered themselves financially able to retire had no wish and no intention of doing so. One 65-year-old man had tried a few years of retirement on doctor's orders but had returned to work:

Mr. H.: I have no desire to quit. I feel that people are much better off if they are working because their mind is better employed at something that you can get some kind of satisfaction out of. It isn't necessarily the money that makes me work. I got a lot ahead and could loaf for quite a while and wouldn't miss any meals at all.

Q. What did you miss most when you weren't working?

A. Well, I wasn't satisfied. I couldn't stay put any place. I used to come over to Chicago and spend a few weeks, my daughter lived here at the time, and then I'd go back to ——, that's where my home is, and I'd go down to Florida and spend maybe two or three months down there. And then down to ——, that was my old home and from there to ——, but I wasn't satisfied any place. So in order to get away from the monotony of loafing, when the job was offered to me, I took it. I have no intention of quitting. If they want to kick me out, they kick me out. Well and good.

Q. Do you think at any time that you will? Maybe not in the natural set of years, but do you think of any time that you might change or that you would want to quit?

A. No, I don't. I was so sick of trying to retire in the four years between 1942 and 1946 that I think that, as long as I'm able to get around on my job, I'm going to be on the job. When I get to a point where I'm not able to carry out my end of it, I hope the Lord takes me off this earth so I won't be a bother to somebody else.

All those who, with or without money, definitely did not wish to retire agreed in general with the following quotations:

Q. Do you think you would miss work if you stopped?

Mrs. D.: Oh, definitely! I would definitely miss it. I don't think I could be very happy if I weren't working. Sometimes you think it would be awfully nice not to have to get up in the morning—and of course all people are different—but for an individual of my type, I don't think I would be very happy if I weren't working. I think it keeps me younger. It keeps me up with so many things that are important in this world of ours. You can't help it if you're out with people, it makes you do it—you have to keep up.

Mr. L.: So the future—I don't let it frighten me at all. Sometimes I do think of it in serious form, but I brush it out of my mind. What the future holds for me I have, oh, I only have a certain percentage of control—because I may be here in five years and I may not. I may be here in twenty-five years. Now we come back to Social Security. Under the present rate possibly the first year will be the hardest, then as my wife comes into Social Security—which will be, I think, a half or two-thirds of what I'm receiving—we might be able to get along on that. I don't know. It depends on what the cost of living is then. So if I can see my advancement or my opportunity of earning more than what my Social Security would give me, I would much rather earn it than take the Social Security. Besides I could always get the Social Security when I'm not able to do anything else. But as long as I'm able I believe I shall always work—until the last.

Q. Would it make any difference if you had a lot of money, say, $50,000 or something like that—or say you had all the money to do anything you wanted to do.

A. If I had, say, $50,000 or all the money that I wanted at the time of my retirement, it may be that I would set myself up in a little business, and the business that I think that I would like mostly would be a little cigar store. You know, cigars and a few little novelties. A few magazines. It would be an easy life for me, there would hardly be a tension, everything will be cash, there will be no bookkeeping. I'd open my store in the morning, and I would close it at night again. I think that's about as easy a way that I know of for a retired man, most particularly if he has a little money, the little profit that he might make on this and the subsidy of the money that he has invested, both together might get along very nicely with a safe security. That would be the type of business I've never been in in my life. It's the type of business that wouldn't require any ingenuity. I still would be meeting people—be meeting them every day. And I would not exert myself. I say there wouldn't be any large amount of bookkeeping and no charge accounts. Everything would be cash. You take in what you put in one pocket and take it out of the other pocket.

Who Wants To Retire

When attitudes toward retirement at age 65 were considered in relation to sex and the meaning of work, it was found
that men in general and people who had extremely high value-of-
work scores did not wish to retire. Those who had extremely low
value-of-work scores wished to retire; but the women were about
equally divided among those who accept, those who reject, and
those with neutral attitudes toward retirement.

Retirement and the Meaning of Work

No relationship was found between any specific meaning of
work and attitudes toward retirement, but a limited relationship
did appear between attitudes toward retirement and the over-all
value of work. That is, those people who recognized and stressed
the most meanings did not want to retire, while those who recognized the fewest meanings and stressed them least did want to
retire.

The value-of-work score was used to check the relationship
between the individual's attitude toward retirement and the number and importance of recognized meanings. These scores ranged
from 1 to 13, in a possible range of 0–21.[4] In the total group those
people who were rated as placing a very high value on work (ten
cases with scores ranging from 11 to 13) expressed a wish to
continue working past the age of 65,[5] except one man who was
"neutral" and one whose attitude was unknown. Conversely,
those who were rated as finding little value in work (six cases
with scores ranging from 1 to 3) expressed a wish to retire at age
65 or before, except one whose attitude was unknown. These
data are shown in Table 14.

Those whose value-of-work scores fell between 4 and 10 split

4. With slight importance = 1, moderate importance = 2, and great importance = 3, a score of 0 would represent no meanings recognized beyond earning
a living; and a score of 21 would represent great importance attached to all
seven meanings.

5. Of those who opposed compulsory retirement at age 65, eight men said
that they would voluntarily retire sometime before they became "too old to
enjoy it." All others, both men and women, who opposed compulsory retirement expressed a wish to continue working as long as they were physically
able to do so.

in their attitudes toward retirement. Of these, twenty-eight did not wish to retire, eleven did, twelve were neutral, and the attitudes of seven were unknown. Neither the combined distribution nor that of men and women considered separately revealed any systematic relationship between attitudes toward retirement and the value-of-work scores in the middle group.

TABLE 14

DISTRIBUTION OF VALUE-OF-WORK SCORES OF MEN
AND WOMEN RELATED TO ATTITUDE TOWARD
RETIREMENT AT AGE 65

ATTITUDE TOWARD RETIREMENT	VALUE-OF-WORK SCORE			
	High (11–13)	Middle (4–10)	Low (1–3)	TOTAL
Men:				
Favorable.........	....	3	3	6
Unfavorable......	5	19	....	4
Neutral..........	1	....	....	1
Unknown.........	1	4	1	6
Women:				
Favorable.........	....	8	2	10
Unfavorable......	3	9	....	12
Neutral..........	....	12	....	12
Unknown.........	....	3	....	3
Total:				
Favorable.........	....	11	5	16
Unfavorable......	8	28	....	36
Neutral..........	1	12	....	13
Unknown.........	1	7	1	9

Thus it appears that, although a relationship can be demonstrated between the meaning of work and attitudes toward retirement for those people who place either extremely high or extremely low value on their work, some other factor or factors must account for the attitudes expressed by the large majority of salespeople who fell within the wide range of the "middle" group as measured by the value-of-work scores. It is possible that, as suggested earlier, the presence or absence of equivalent satisfactions in the individuals' nonwork life is the factor which would account for these varying attitudes toward retirement, whatever the value of work to the individual.

Are Women More Willing To Retire than Men?

The saleswomen, in general, considered retirement more favorably than the salesmen. However, they did not express this preference as clearly as expected; instead they split almost equally among the three categories.

The differences in the distribution of men and women according to their attitudes toward retirement, shown in Table 14, are quite marked. Of the total group of men, two-thirds definitely wished to keep on working; one-sixth wished to retire; and only one person expressed a neutral attitude. Slightly more than a third of the women wished to keep on working; less than a third wished to retire; and slightly more than a third were neutral.

In spite of the relatively high number of women who wished to continue working, the expected differences between the sexes can be seen in the fact that the ratio of those who wished to work compared with those who wished to retire was approximately one to one for the women and four to one for the men.

The large number of women who expressed neutral attitudes, or a willingness to accept equally work or retirement, can be viewed in two ways. First, in strict comparison with the negative stand toward retirement of the great majority of the men, it shows a greater willingness on the part of the women to retire. On the other hand, with respect to the general expectation that these women might feel that their rightful place is in the home, it shows an unexpected willingness on their part to work.

The fact that women as a group accept retirement more readily than men is probably explained, as suggested early in the study, by the fact that they do have an alternative role which is acceptable or attractive to many. The unexpectedly large number of women who did not actually wish to retire is probably related to the fact that, contrary to expectation, women found as many meanings in work as men did and that they stressed them as heavily. It was suggested when this finding was discussed that women, having had the opportunity to contrast a working life with home life, actually found work to be varied, challenging, and interesting and their home life restricted and dull by comparison. Apparently many women are faced with the same problem as most men;

and, even though they have an acceptable role in society besides that of worker, they themselves may find it inadequate for their needs and interests.

SUMMARY AND CONCLUSIONS

In this chapter we have tried to answer four questions: (1) Do salespeople recognize and stress heavily many meanings of work beyond earning a living? (2) Do women value work less than men do? (3) Is there a relationship between attitudes toward retirement at age 65 and the meaning of work? (4) Are women more willing to retire at age 65 than men?

The interviews showed that the salespeople in general attached considerable importance to a great variety of meanings; that women valued their work as much as the men; that those who placed extremely high value on work did not wish to retire; and that women as a group showed greater willingness to retire than men. At the same time, these findings raised the following questions: (1) Why did the women value work so much more than was expected? (2) Why were extreme value-of-work scores related to attitudes toward retirement and other scores not? (3) Why were so many more women than expected eager or willing to continue work?

For each of these questions it was suggested that the answer depended upon whether or not the individual had satisfactions and interests outside of work with which to replace those found in work. This suggestion can be tested by reviewing certain interviews in detail to find out whether or not the interviewees themselves told of circumstances in their nonwork life which confirm or refute it. Three relatively small groups will serve this purpose: (1) those with extremely high value-of-work scores; (2) those with extremely low value-of-work scores; and (3) other men who wished to retire.

Reference to the interviews of the three women and six men who valued their work highly reveals similarities in personality, in that they talked readily, vividly, and at length with very little questioning. With all these people, enjoyment and appreciation of the many facets of their work was obvious, and all expressed the feeling that nothing outside their work life could offer the rewards and satisfactions they found in their jobs.

On the other hand, those who placed the lowest value on work, with one exception, had little to say about their work, themselves, and their experiences. Aside from this generalization, they had very little in common in their personalities. Among the men, one was in a highly nervous state, possibly ill; the second said that "naturally" he would like to retire—just to work around the house—but he would probably miss the people; the third, and most freely talkative, was an artist-craftsman who had given up his work during the war and was working as a salesman until he should be eligible for Social Security, at which time he planned to devote full time to his craft. Both of the women in this group were widows. One quite poignantly wished for marriage and home life; the other expressed at some length, but in a matter-of-fact manner, her feeling that a woman's place is primarily in the home and that she would not work if she did not have to.

Among the other men who wished to retire, the lowest ranking according to the value-of-work scores saw work as a routine way to keep busy and said that, if retired, he "would have lots to do around the house." The second, medium in the value-of-work scale, is a man who has a hobby which he carries on at home and which he says is his "first love." The third, whose score was quite high, had already become part owner of a small business in the North, was planning to make similar arrangements in the South, and expected to divide his time between the two places when he retired.

In these three cases as well as in the three that ranked lowest according to the value-of-work scores, every man who wished to retire was found to have more absorbing interests outside his job or to give evidence of a general low level of activity, and each was prepared to follow up interests in retirement which were markedly similar to his job as he saw it in the degree of activity, variety, and challenge they offered. The two women who valued work least and who actively wished to retire placed a high value on home life and felt that work kept them from their desired satisfactions.

Thus the available evidence indicates that the presence or absence of equivalent satisfactions outside the work life also is related to attitudes toward retirement and may be the most important factor. At any rate, it seems that the relationships between sex, an extremely high or extremely low valuation of work, and attitudes toward retirement can best be understood in this context.

V

The Meanings of Work for Skilled Craftsmen

Our first investigation of the meanings of work was a mail questionnaire study of a group of skilled craftsmen 65 years and over who had the option of retiring or continuing at their jobs full time when they reached their sixty-fifth birthday. In this initial exploratory investigation we wanted to (1) assess the meanings which these workers assigned to their jobs; (2) determine their views toward retirement; (3) investigate the relation between the meanings assigned to work and the decision to retire; and (4) develop an approach which would be useful in exploring this area of life-experience over a wide range of occupations and skills.

THE GROUP SELECTED AND THE STUDY HYPOTHESES

The study group was composed of all members 65 years and over of the Chicago local of a small craft union in the printing trades. These are highly skilled, well-paid male workers who belong to an old and traditionally skilled craft.

Although this craft combines the ancient European printer's art with modern American technology, the nature of the product is such that mass-production techniques have not yet been successfuly adapted. Each item has its own design and execution problems, requiring the personal supervision of the craftsman. For many tasks, artistic ability of a fairly high order is needed. Thus, the workers are both skilled artisans and skilled technicians —enjoying both the artisan's traditional pride of craft and the relatively high status assigned to the technician in an industrial society.

132

Because of the strong position the union has occupied in the industry, it has been able to maintain a tight control over the labor supply, striving always to prevent an oversupply of skilled labor which would weaken its bargaining position. The craft has, consequently, been a difficult one to get into, and, because of a required six-year apprenticeship, it seems to have weeded out the "casual" or "indifferent" workman. Once accepted as journeymen, these men remain in the trade a long time, 83 per cent of them having thirty years or more service, 70 per cent having forty years in the trade, and 33 per cent with fifty or more years service. Combining the tradition, status, high pay, tight organization, sense of being selected, and long training and period of service typical of these men, we would expect to find a group that represents the elite of the skilled craft movement.

These, then, were largely jobs at which men chose to work. In fact, when they were asked what they would have done at age 40 if they had all the money they needed, 72 per cent of the group stated that they would have continued working at the same jobs they had. Similarly, when asked what line of work they would advise a young man to go into today, 60 per cent suggested a skilled trade in preference to business or a profession.

This trade is also unique in that it has no compulsory retirement requirements. The worker upon reaching the age of 65 has his choice of retiring or of continuing full-time employment in his trade. Of the workers over 65, 111 were employed full time at their craft and 113 had retired. Few men drew pensions from their employers, but practically all were entitled to a union allotment of $10 a week plus Social Security benefits. If these men wanted to continue work past 65, they seemed to have little difficulty obtaining employment as long as they were able to do their job. Nor was the older worker unwelcome in the shop. Employers seemed to consider favorably these men's skill and fund of experiencee. In many cases they were looked to for advice on technical problems, and in some cases increased age brought a position of increased prestige as the "deans" of the shop.

Thus we have a group of highly skilled artisans, many of whom might be able to afford retirement at age 65, who were given the chance to continue full-time employment in their trade.

It seemed as though we had an excellent group for an initial study of the meaning of work and its relation to both attitude toward retirement and the decision to retire.

The Study Hypotheses

The following hypotheses were devised to test the relations between the meanings of work, as we have presented the construct, and these skilled workers' attitudes toward retirement and decision to retire:

I. *Work has meanings in addition to that of earning a living for this group of workers.* These nonfinancial, or extra-economic, meanings of work center around the job as a source of self-respect and the respect of others, as association, as routine, and as a source of meaningful life-experience.

II. *Most members of this craft who are of retirement age tend to stress the extra-economic meanings of work to a greater extent than its economic meaning.* This is based on the assumption that in the course of a lifetime of work at this trade the individual's scheme of life-organization has become "involved" in the performance of his job to a greater extent than could be accounted for on the basis of income alone and that in this craft the extra-economic considerations take precedence for most workers over income.

III. *Those men who stress the extra-economic meanings of work will hold a less favorable attitude toward retirement than those men who regard work as primarily a way to earn a living.*

IV. *Those men who stress the extra-economic meanings of work will prefer to continue at their jobs past "normal" retirement age, even thought they are financially able to retire.*

V. *Those men who regard work as primarily a way of earning a living will prefer to retire at "normal" retirement age or as soon after as they can afford it.*

THE STUDY DESIGN

The Study Instrument

Union officials would not allow an interview study of their membership at their homes, nor did they favor the use of the union meetings or offices for personal administration of a schedule. At the union's request, a study questionnaire was drawn up to be distributed by mail. A combination of check list and open-ended questions was used in an effort to get the following types of information pertinent to our study:

1. General
   a) Age
   b) Nativity
   c) Education
   d) Health
   e) Economic status
2. Work status
   a) Number of years as skilled craftsman
   b) Employed or retired
   c) Length of time since last employed
3. Evaluation of the skilled craft as a career
   a) Job advice to be given to young man today
   b) Work choice at age 40, if could afford to retire
4. Meaning of work
   a) Meaning-of-work check list
   b) Factors missed about job upon retirement
   c) Attitude toward work
   d) Like most about work
   e) Like least about work
5. Attitude toward retirement
   a) Age of expected retirement at age 55
   b) Conditions under which a man ought to retire
   c) Attitude toward retirement
   d) Retirement plans
   e) Work choice at age 65
   f) Meaning of retirement
   g) Retirement anxieties
6. The decision to continue work
   a) Expected and preferred retirement ages
   b) Reason for continuing work
   c) Amount of thought given to retirement
   d) Expected financial position upon retirement
7. The decision to retire
   a) Age of retirement
   b) Reason for retirement
   c) Like most about retirement
   d) Like least about retirement

The questionnaire was pretested by personal administration to a small number of workers and by extensive consultation with union officials as to the appropriateness and particular connotations of the questions for this group of workers.

Returns to the Questionnaire

The questionnaire was distributed by mail under union auspices to all members, employed and retired, 65 years of age and over. A follow-up mailing was made to all members who had not responded after a two-week interval. These two mailings obtained completed questionnaires from 172 of the 224 members solicited, or 77 per cent of the study universe. This 77 per cent response represented 92 per cent of the retired men and 68 per cent[1] of the employed.

A subsample of 14 of the 43 nonrespondents in the employed group was then drawn for follow up. Intensive solicitation produced 11 responses, bringing the gross employed response up to 71 per cent and the gross total up to 82 per cent. However, if we assign a weight of 3 to each of the 11 replies to the one-third sample of the employed group nonrespondents, we have a weighted response total of 91 per cent for the employed and 91 per cent for the entire group (see Table 15).

TABLE 15

AGE AND EMPLOYMENT STATUS
OF PARTICIPANTS

Age	Employed	Retired	Total
65–69............	89*	42	110*
70–74............	26*	43	69*
75–79............	5	17	22
80 and over......	....	5	5
Total........	101*	107	208*

* Weighted total.

RESPONSE BIAS AND TESTS OF SIGNIFICANCE

Our maximum bias due to nonrespondents would be 8 per cent for the retired men, 9 per cent for the employed, and 9 per cent for the group as a whole. Although we are dealing with all members of a completely listed universe (i.e., all members 65 years and over of this union local), we can regard this group as a sample in the sense that it is a sample of this group in time. We cannot assume that the composition of the universe would have been the same if the study were conducted one month or one year, for example, before or after the date it was undertaken. To the extent that we can assume that these variations would be random, we can apply tests of significance based upon random sample theory to our findings. In this case we have used the test for the significance of difference of percentages for all compari-

1. It should be noted that the mailings were made in July, when perhaps 10–15 per cent of the employed men were on vacation.

sons of findings commented upon in our text. In general, a difference of 10–12 per cent proved to be significant at the 5 per cent level.

THE MEANINGS OF WORK

"Earning a living" was selected by 84 per cent of the group from a check list of the meanings of work included in the questionnaire. Only 14 per cent of the group replied to the question without acknowledging the economic meaning of work. And 22 per cent of the group indicated no meaning for work other than that of earning a living.

However, 76 per cent of the group indicated that work had come to have meanings in their lives other than or in addition to its defined economic function. Self-respect and the respect of others, being with and working with others, and a chance to be creative were the most frequently selected of the extra-economic meanings of work (Table 16).

In addition to checking the meanings which their work has had for them, the subjects were also asked to rank the meanings in terms of their first and second degree of importance (see Table 17). Fifty-six per cent of the respondents rated a way of earning a living as the most important meaning of work, and 23 per cent selected meanings other than that of earning a living. Self-respect was selected by more than half of the respondents who ranked the extra-economic meanings of work as most important for them.

Forty-five per cent of the group listed a second choice as well. Work as "filling the day and giving something to do," as a source of "self-respect," and as a "chance to be with and work with others" were the most frequently chosen second choices.

Considering the meanings of work in terms of the subjects' own rating of their importance, we find earning a living stressed as first choice about twice as often as all the other meanings combined. If we combine the first and second choices, we find that the three meanings of work other than that of earning a living which were rated as most important were: self-respect, a chance to be creative, and a way of filling the day and having something

TABLE 16

FREQUENCY OF OCCURRENCE OF THE MEANINGS OF WORK

MEANING OF WORK	EMPLOYED		RETIRED		TOTAL	
	No.	Per Cent	No.	Per Cent	No.	Per Cent
1. Earning a living	81	80	94	88	175	84
2. Filling the day and offering something to do	29	29	35	33	64	31
3, *a* and *b*. Self-respect and the respect of others	46	46	58	54	104	50
4. Being with and working with others	34	34	50	47	84	40
5, *b*. Chance to be creative	38	38	35	33	73	35
5, *c*. Source of new experience	27	27	29	27	56	27
No reply	4	4	1	1	5	2

TABLE 17

THE MEANINGS OF WORK FOR 101 EMPLOYED AND 107 RETIRED SKILLED CRAFTSMEN

MEANING OF WORK	EMPLOYED		RETIRED		PER CENT OF TOTAL NO.	
	First Choice	Second Choice	First Choice	Second Choice	First Choice	Second Choice
1. Earning a living	55	6	61	7	56	6
2. Filling the day and offering something to do	1	19	1	10	1	14
3, *a*.* Self-respect / 3, *b*.* The respect of others	16	8	15	15	15	11
4. Being with and working with others	2	4	5	10	3	7
5, *b*. Chance to be creative	6	5	4	5	5	5
5, *c*. Source of new experience	1	2	......	3	......	2
Total making choices	81	44	86	50	167	94

* Since there were some indications that these two alternatives were used interchangeably by the subjects, we have combined them into a single category.

TABLE 18

RANKINGS OF THE MEANINGS OF WORK BY FREQUENCY OF OCCURRENCE AND RELATIVE DEGREE OF STRESS

MEANING OF WORK	FREQUENCY			STRESS		
	Employed	Retired	Total	Employed	Retired	Total
1. Earning a living	1	1	1	1	1	1
3, *a* and *b*. Self-respect and the respect of others	2	2	2	2	2	2
4. Being with and working with others	4	3	3	5	5	5
5, *b*. Chance to be creative	3	4	4	3	3	3
2. Filling the day and having something to do	5	4	5	3	3	3
5, *d*. Source of new experience	6	6	6	6	6	6

to do. In addition to these three meanings, the retired men also stressed work "as a chance to be and work with others."

If we combine the two forms of the tabulation, we can compare the ordering of the frequency of occurrence and the relative degree of stress of the meanings of work among this group of workers (see Table 18).

Our hypothesis that work had come to have meanings other than that of earning a living seems to have been borne out. However, we failed to substantiate the hypothesis that these meanings were stressed to a greater extent by this group of skilled craftsmen than earning a living. In terms both of its frequency of occurrence in the group and of the stress laid upon it by the individual worker, earning a living was the basic meaning which their jobs held for them.

Earning a living is society's rationale for working at a job. Even where other meanings were found, many of these were expressed in terms of earning a living. As one respondent wrote, commenting upon the question: "My work has given me income without which I could have neither self-respect nor the respect of others."

Whereas income was the key to why these men worked at a job, it is perhaps the other meanings which they assigned to their work that describe the part which their particular jobs had come to play in their lives. Self-respect was the most important of the extra-economic meanings of work reported by these craftsmen, being listed by 50 per cent and rated as the most important meaning by 12 per cent. Self-respect here refers to the status accorded to a skilled craftsman in the community as well as the recognition obtained in the work group and the family. The job was apparently one of their own choosing for many of them, one which they would choose again if they could live their lives over again, and one which they would strongly recommend to a young man today. It is regarded as one of the more desirable jobs which society has to offer.

About 40 per cent of the group regarded work as association, as a chance to be with and work with others. Association here refers to the fellow-worker relationships which exist on the job itself and also may include relationships with other workers of their craft away from the job as well. Although it ranked third in frequence of occurrence, it only ranked fifth in degree of stress laid upon it and probably can be considered a meaning which is generally recognized by these workers but not regarded as an important aspect of their jobs.

Although work as a "chance to be creative" and as "filling the day and offering something to do" were selected by somewhat smaller proportions of the group, they received a greater degree of stress by individuals reporting them than did association. Perhaps the distinctive character, the flavor of work experience in this skilled craft, is reflected in the nature of this work as "meaningful life-experience," which ranked next to self-respect in frequency of occurrence. Here we find revealed the craftsman who commands the sense of creativity and accomplishment of the artisan in his work. The worker is matched against the materials and by his skill and ingenuity creates a purposeful object out of an inanimate mass.

Routine was of relatively little importance among the meanings associated with working at this skilled trade. There is little in the job itself that requires repetitive automatic action. The routine referred to may also include the habit of being at a fixed place during a fixed set of hours five days a week and also the habit of making the trip to and from the place of work.

Attitude toward Retirement and the Meaning of Work

Of course a man sure does miss to some extent the business life he had before retirement, and he must make new conditions for himself. The time does not seem so long as some feel because I do something every day—one thing or another. At home for my wife, I help wherever I can. I know that I can't work at my trade any more, but life is not useless to me. I look around me and see how things in nature are getting old, but they go on just the same. Old age is something no one can escape. I say, "prepare for it." It is inevitable for all. [Comment on retirement inclosed with questionnaire of a retired worker.]

We were unable to characterize this group of craftsmen— either its employed or retired members, or the group as a whole— by any single expression of opinion toward retirement. Nor for the group as a whole were we able to support our hypothesis that "those men who stress the 'extra-economic' meanings of work will hold a less favorable attitude toward retirement than the men who regard work as primarily a way of earning a living." The hypothesis did hold true for the employed group, although not for the retired.

We found that among the employed group—in keeping with our hypothesis—those men who stressed the extra-economic meanings of work reported retirement as "the worst thing that could happen to a man," indicated a desire to remain at their jobs past age 65, and viewed retirement as having fewer positive satisfactions to a significantly although not enormously greater extent than did the men who stressed work as primarily a way of earning a living. However, among the retired men the reverse of our proposition proved to be true; that is, those men who stressed the extra-economic meanings of work regarded retirement more favorably than did the retired men for whom work was primarily a way of earning a living.

Our hypothesis in effect equated the stressing of the extra-economic meanings of work with an unfavorable view of retirement. Implicit in this hypothesis is the assumption that the extra-economic meanings and satisfactions of the job are not readily replaced in retirement. And on the basis of our findings this may have been a factor in influencing the attitude toward retirement of 38 per cent of the employed men who had emphasized the extra-economic meanings of their job (compared with about 19 per cent of the total employed group). However, retirement itself could not have been entirely a "functionless" situation for them. Fifty-six per cent of the group of retired men who had stressed the extra-economic factors in their job, presumably the group that would suffer most keenly from the loss of the work function, reported that retirement was a satisfactory experience for them.

The Decision To Continue Work Past Retirement Age

We were studying the members of a trade in which retirement at age 65 or after was an optional choice for most; about half of the workers over 65 had retired, and half had elected to remain at their jobs. We then had the opportunity of relating the meaning of work not only to the subject's attitude toward retirement but also to his actual behavior in the situation where he was called upon to decide whether he wanted to retire or continue work. As in the case of attitudes toward retirement, we found that our hypothesis concerning the relation of the meaning of work and the decision to retire received support among the men who were remaining at their jobs but did not apply to the retired men.

In the case of the employed men, we found our hypotheses that "those men who stress the extra-economic meanings of work will prefer to continue at their jobs past 'normal' retirement age, even though they are financially able to retire" and that "those men who regard work as primarily a way of earning a living will prefer to retire at 'normal' retirement age, or as soon after as they can afford it," received strong support. Of the men who were currently employed, about half indicated that they had remained at their jobs past "normal" retirement age because they needed the income which their jobs provided, and half indicated that they remained for reasons other than that of financial need. Of the group which stated that they remained at their jobs for reasons other than that of financial need, 44 per cent stressed the extra-economic meanings of work as compared with 12 per cent of the men who listed financial need as the reason for remaining, and 76 per cent indicated that they would miss factors other than income most about their jobs if they were to retire as compared with only 19 per cent of the men who stated they remained at their jobs because of financial need. We also have some positive but inconclusive evidence to indicate that the group which remained at the job for reasons other than that of financial need was actually in a better financial position than which continued because they needed the income and that some of them at least probably could have afforded to retire. And, further, we found that the group which indicated that they remained at their jobs for reasons other than financial need also evidenced a negative view of retirement, gave reasons other than that of financial need, and indicated major concerns about retirement unrelated to the problem of subsistence of maintaining their standard of living, all to a significantly greater extent than the group which stated that they had remained at the job because they needed the income.

The Decision To Retire

My hope of retirement was really inspired by the advent of Social Security. Then union assistance together with several prosperous years and high wages made withdrawing from the workaday world—with its noise and confusion—possible. There were many things I had long been interested in—useful things—that I only lacked time to cultivate. I needed lots of time. So my plans just gradually worked themselves out. The plans worked me. When I first entertained the idea of retirement, my income seemed ample. With no rent, and a garden to raise much of our food, and clothes a reduced necessity, I thought that coal, taxes, groceries, and upkeep of the house would be the only costly items. But the prices of all these have risen, and there were dozens of expenditures I had not reckoned with. We are still "getting by" in comfort but hope that costs will not continue to rise. [Comment on retirement inclosed with questionnaire of retired worker.]

We failed to get an adequate response to our question as to why these workers retired. The decision to retire had already been made by all this group; for most it was a decision that had been made some years past. However, in response to questions which attempted to get them to define their present position, we found what seems to be two different views of the nature of the retirement process itself—views which the men may have held prior to their actual retirement. One group, 48 per cent, regarded retirement as something which had been done to them—a permanent separation from their jobs which had been forced upon them. They had been retired from their work. The other group, 41 per cent, seemed to regard themselves as *having retired;* that is, as having entered retirement at least willingly if not voluntarily. This latter group appeared to be in better health (not forced to retire because of health) and in a somewhat more secure financial position (better able to retire). There were indications that some members of this group would have retired earlier but were asked to continue working through World War II because of the shortage of men in their craft. Perhaps it was the income gained during the war years, income which could be added to what they had already set aside for retirement, which made retirement a more readily accepted experience for them. However, we were not able to distinguish between these two groups in terms of the distinctive meanings these workers attached to their jobs or in terms of their stressing of the extra-economic as compared with the economic meaning of work.

Although we have no direct evidence on the relation of the meaning of work to the decision to retire, we did find a difference in the relation of the meaning of work and attitude toward retirement in the two groups described above. In general, the group which regarded itself as having retired viewed retirement much more favorably than the group which regarded itself as having been retired. More specifically, we discovered that within the group which defined itself as having retired we found a more pronounced tendency for the men who stressed the extra-economic meanings of work to regard retirement favorably than among the members of the group who stressed work as a way of earning a living. Thus, not only have we failed to show that the retired men for whom the extra-economic meanings of work have been important are reluctant to accept retirement but we actually have some evidence to indicate that they regard retirement more favorably than those workers for whom the job has been primarily a way of earning a living.

VI

Change with Age in the Meanings of Work
for Skilled Craftsmen

THE general problem of this study was to investigate the views of a 20–64 age group about retirement in the attempt to gain some insight into and understanding of what meanings work may have in a worker's life. A mailed questionnaire was employed to elicit responses from a sample of highly skilled workers in one of the printing trades. An analysis was then undertaken of these responses in order to see what meanings were assigned to work.

The present study attempted to test two hypotheses. First, highly skilled workers stress meanings of work other than that of earning a living. Second, the meanings of work vary according to the age and marital status of individuals within a given skill level. Only two of the many aspects investigated by the original questionnaire were used to test these hypotheses. One of the questions is concerned with what work means in general to the worker. The other deals with things about his work which a worker will miss most when he retires.

DESIGN OF THE STUDY

The original sample of 516 workers was drawn from a total group of 1,583 union local members. To avoid a confounding of factors, foreign-born workers[1] and divorced and widowed workers were eliminated from the study group.[2] The sampling design, with an adequate number of cases to yield satisfactory results, is

1. About 10 per cent of the union membership under 65 years of age was foreign-born.

2. Divorced and widowed workers were dropped from the total group (and later from the sample of respondents as they were disclosed) because there was no way of determining, except by individual case study, whether the

145

indicated in Table 19. The number of respondents to two administrations of the questionnaire and to a special follow-up
study of a 10 per cent sample of nonrespondents is also shown.[3]

THE MEANINGS OF WORK

The workers were asked to indicate what meaning or meanings
work has had for them.[4] The results are presented in terms of the

TABLE 19

RESPONDENTS TO THE TWO ADMINISTRATIONS OF THE QUESTIONNAIRE AND
THE FOLLOW-UP STUDY OF NONRESPONDENTS

Age and Marital Status	No. of Cases in Universe	Per Cent Sampling Ratio	Expected No. of Cases	Total No. of Respondents	Per Cent of Sample Responding	Per Cent of Universe Reached
Married:						
Under 45........	768	10	79	52	65.8	6.8
45–54..........	410	20	82	38	46.4	9.3
55–64..........	246	100	244	120	49.2	48.8
Nonmarried:						
Under 45........	89	50	43	13	30.2	14.6
45 and over......	70	100	68	19	28.0	27.1
Total........	1,583	....	516	242	46.9	....

financial obligations of such workers placed them in the category of married
or of single workers and whether their marital experiences might have in-
fluenced the ways in which they regard their work and eventual retirement.

3. Within each of the subcategories where less than a 100 per cent sample
was taken, a systematic sample was drawn with a random start. However,
because of the large number of nonrespondents and because of the number
of cases within the sample which had to be excluded, it was impossible to
consider the remaining cases as a representative sample. It was possible to use
the questionnaires of only 242 respondents, or 46.9 per cent of the original
sample. All further discussion is based upon the analysis of these 242 cases.
No attempt can be made to extend these findings in order to generalize about
the union local or the entire craft, much less to skilled workers in general.

4. The questionnaire contained the item:
"What meanings does work have for you in life (*please check all items that
apply to you*):
"1. My work has given me self-respect. ....   ———.
"2. My work has given me the respect of others ....   ———.
"3. My work has given me the chance to be with and to work with
     people ....   ———.
"4. My work has been only a way of earning a living ....   ———.
"5. My work has given me a chance to be creative ....   ———.
"6. My work at the shop is a source of new experience ....   ———.
"(*If you have had more than one choice, mark your first choice 1.*)"

numbers of first choices assigned to each meaning and the frequency of choice of each statement regardless of its ranking. The rankings the workers assigned to other statements when certain statements were indicated as first choice are also presented to help interpret the significance of the frequencies of first choices for some of the statements. Finally, the results are given in terms of how many married and single workers in each age group ranked the various statements as first, second, third, etc., choice.

Table 20 shows the frequency of occurrence of choices and

TABLE 20

RANKING AND TOTAL NUMBER OF CHOICES OF THE STATEMENTS DEALING WITH THE MEANING OF WORK, BY AGE AND MARITAL STATUS

STATEMENT	RANK	MARRIED				SINGLE		TOTAL NO. OF CHOICES
		Under 45	45–54	55–59	60–64	Under 45	55–64	
My work has given me self-respect	1	18	18	18	18	6	4	77
	2	4	1	2	3	......	1	11
	3	1	......	1	......	1	......	3
	Other	......	......	......	......	......	......	......
My work has given me the respect of others	1	5	5	2	3	1	......	16
	2	7	2	4	3	1	......	17
	3	1	......	1	3	......	1	6
	Other	1	3	......	1	1	......	6
My work has given me the chance to be with and to work with people	1	2	2	9	2	2	1	18
	2	4	1	4	1	......	1	11
	3	7	5	3	2	2	......	19
	Other	3	1	......	1	1	1	7
My work has been only a way of earning a living	1	8	4	14	11	3	2	42
	2	2	2	1	1	......	1	7
	3	......	......	......	1	......	......	1
	Other	2	1	......	......	......	......	3
My work has given me a chance to be creative	1	8	2	5	2	3	3	23
	2	3	4	2	2	1	1	13
	3	2	1	1	1	......	......	5
	Other	3	2	3	1	1	......	10
My work at the shop is a source of new experience	1	2	3	2	......	2	......	9
	2	2	1	1	......	1	1	6
	3	3	2	1	......	......	......	6
	Other	3	5	2	2	......	......	12
Total no. of choices...		......	......	......	......	......	......	328
Total no. of workers making choices.....		55	38	71	49	22	10	242

the rankings for the six statements dealing with the meaning of work. Of the 242 respondents, 185 indicated first choices. More workers answered the question than the results indicate. However, only those cases were included in which the respondent made some effort to rank the statements. Of the 185 workers who indicated first choices, 77 assigned this choice to "My work has given me self-respect." Of the remaining 108 first choices, 42 were given to "My work has been only a way of earning a living." These results support the hypothesis that highly skilled workers stress meanings of work other than its being only a way of earning a living.

A total of 328 choices was made by the 185 respondents. The statement, "My work has given me self-respect," received the greatest number of choices (91) and the highest rankings; while "My work at the shop is a source of new experience" received the least number of choices, one-third of which were ranked fourth or fifth. The remaining statements received about an equal number of total choices.

Only about one-sixth (53) of the total choices were given to the statement, "My work has been only a way of earning a living." This result indicates that the group of respondents stress meanings of work other than that of earning a living. Further, there is some indication of a tentative ordering of meanings that work has for this group. In descending order, these meanings may be listed as self-respect, association, earning a living, the opportunity to be creative, and the intrinsic nature of the work situation. This ordering is based on the total number of choices made for each statement. No attempt was made in this question to have the workers indicate from what point of view they were considering work. Some may have been thinking of it in terms of their financial or family obligations and responsibilities; others in terms of job satisfaction or a host of other factors.

a) The relationship between first and second choices.—In order to see how the workers ranked the statements in relation to each other, the results were arranged to show the number of second choices given to all of the statements when each was ranked first (Table 21). For example, of the 77 workers who ranked "My work has given me self-respect" as their first choice, 14 indicated "My work has given me the respect of others" as second choice, and 8 workers chose "My work has given me the chance to be with and to work with people." Many possible explanations may be made of these results. One is that this clustering may indicate a common element running through these statements. It is suggested that this common element may be that many workers

TABLE 21

THE MEANING OF WORK: THE NUMBER OF SECOND CHOICES GIVEN TO ALL STATEMENTS WHEN EACH STATEMENT IS RANKED FIRST

STATEMENT	NO. OF FIRST CHOICES	STATEMENT AND NUMBER OF SECOND CHOICES					
		My work has given me self-respect	My work has given me the respect of others	My work has given me the chance to be with and to work with people	My work has been only a way of earning a living	My work has given me a chance to be creative	My work at the shop is a source of new experience
My work has given me self-respect.........	77		14	8	3	9	....
My work has given me the respect of others.	16	1		....	3	1	....
My work has given me the chance to be with and to work with people........	18	....	1		1	1	....
My work has been only a way of earning a living	42	7	....	3		2	1
My work has given me a chance to be creative..	23	3	1	....	....		5
My work at the shop is a source of new experience.........	9	....	1	....	....	....	

view their work in terms of the status it affords them among their peers. The fact that 9 workers gave second choice to "My work has given me a chance to be creative" also suggests that self-respect may be related to the praise accorded a worker by his fellows because of his creative abilities. On the other hand, of the 42 workers who indicated as first choice "My work has been only a way of earning a living," 7 gave as their second choice "My work has given me the chance to be with and to work with people." This suggests that many workers only conceive of their work in economic terms.

Five of the 23 workers who ranked "My work has given me a chance to be creative" first gave second choice to "My work at the shop is a source of new experience"; and 3 gave second choice to "My work has given me self-respect." This may indicate that, to some workers, work is a manifestation of what Thorstein Veblen termed the "instinct of workmanship." They probably value their shopwork in terms of the new creative experiences they encounter there, while their work gives them increased self-respect because of the opportunity afforded them to express their creative abilities. This response is not surprising when one bears in mind that their trade requires a very high degree of manual skill and artistic ability. Many persons having a well-developed creative urge would be attracted to such an occupation.

b) The ranking of statements by age and marital status.—To determine what variations occurred by age and marital status, the results were arranged according to the rankings given to each statement by the married and single workers. These rankings are also shown in Table 20.

Self-respect may be regarded as the most common meaning that work has for the particular group of workers studied, regardless of their age or marital status. However, the secondary rankings of the statements dealing with the meanings of work appear to be affected by these variables. These rankings lend support to the hypothesis that the meanings of work vary according to the age and marital status of individuals within a given skill level.

For example, married workers of all ages gave the greatest number of first choices to "My work has given me self-respect." Married workers under 45 years of age gave the second largest number of first choices equally to "My work has been only a way of earning a living" and "My work has given me a chance to be creative." Married workers 45–54 years of age gave the second largest number of first choices to "My work has given me the respect of others." The married group 55–64 years of age gave their second largest number of first choices to "My work has been only a way of earning a living." Among the single workers, those under 55 years of age gave the second largest number of first choices equally to "My work has been only a way of earning a living" and "My work has given me a chance to be creative." The single workers 55 years of age and over gave their second largest number of first choices to "My work has given me a chance to be creative." Thus, no consistent pattern of variation of meanings with age was observed among the married workers. However, it would seem that among single workers the importance of work as an opportunity to be creative may increase with age.

What Workers Think They Will Miss Most When They Retire

To test the hypothesis further, the workers were asked to indicate what they thought they would miss most about their work when they retired.[5] Once again the results are presented in terms of the numbers of first choices given to each statement and the frequency of choice of each statement regardless of its ranking.

Table 22 shows the frequency of occurrence of choices and the rankings for the six statements dealing with what workers think they will miss most when they retire. Only 195 of the 242 respondents indicated first choices. More workers answered the question than the results indicate. However, only those cases were included where the respondent made some attempt to rank the statements. On these 195 workers, 93 assigned first choice to "The wages," and 15 indicated "Having to give up things I do now because of lower income." When this group of workers indicated what they would miss most about their work when they retired, the economic factor was stressed most commonly.

A total of 490 choices were made by the 195 respondents. The statement, "The wages," received the greatest number of choices (127). It was followed closely by the statements, "Being with my

5. The questionnaire contained the item:
"What do you think you will miss most when you retire? Check as many items as you wish and mark the most important item (1), the next important (2), etc.
"1. Being with my friends at work .... ———.
"2. The wages .... ———.
"3. Enjoyment of the work itself .... ———.
"4. The feeling of being creative .... ———.
"5. Having to give up things I do now because of lower income .... ———.
"6. The feeling of having something to do with my time .... ———.

friends at work" (105 choices) and "Enjoyment of the work itself" (95 choices). However, it is probable that the statement, "Having to give up things I do now because of lower income" (63 choices), is a further reflection of the economic factor involved in "The wages." Hence, it is considered advisable to treat these two statements together and to assign 190 choices to the economic element. About two-fifths of the total number of

TABLE 22

RANKING AND TOTAL NUMBER OF CHOICES OF THE STATEMENTS DEALING
WITH WHAT 242 WORKERS WILL MISS MOST WHEN THEY RETIRE

Statement	No. Selecting This Category as First Choice	Per Cent of Total Group	No. Selecting This Category as Second Choice	Per Cent of Total Group	Total No. of Responses to Each Category	Per Cent of Total Group
Being with my friends at work..................	34	14	39	16	105	43
The wages..............	93	38	21	8	127	52
Enjoyment of the work itself.................	27	11	37	15	95	39
The feeling of being creative	21	9	22	9	65	27
Having to give up things I do now because of lower income...............	15	6	26	11	73	30
The feeling of having something to do with my time	5	2	9	4	35	14

choices were assigned to the economic factor, while the next largest number of choices (about one-quarter) were for "Being with my friends at work." These results tend to support the hypothesis that highly skilled workers stress meanings of work other than its being only a way of earning a living.

There is also some indication of a tentative ordering of things which workers will miss most about their work when they retire, namely, income, friends, the intrinsic nature of the work situation, the opportunity to be creative, and self-respect, in descending order of importance. This ordering differs in many respects from the ordering obtained when the worker was asked to rank the meanings of work. The fact that so few workers indicate they will have to give up anything because of lower income or that they believe they will have too much time on their hands suggests that most of the workers have given little or no consideration to possible changes in role and the possible loss of self-respect due to their lowered incomes and increased leisure time.

a) *The relationship between first and second choices.*—To ascertain how the workers ranked the statements in relation to each other, the results were arranged to show the number of second choices given to all the statements when each was ranked first (Table 23). For example, of the 93 workers who ranked

TABLE 23

WHAT WORKERS WILL MISS MOST WHEN THEY RETIRE: THE NUMBER OF SECOND CHOICES GIVEN TO ALL STATEMENTS WHEN EACH STATEMENT IS RANKED FIRST

STATEMENT	No. of First Choices	STATEMENT AND NUMBER OF FIRST CHOICES					
		Being with my friends at work	The wages	Enjoyment of the work itself	The feeling of being creative	Having to give up things I do now because of lower income	The feeling of having something to do with my time
Being with my friends at work	34		9	9	6	1	....
The wages	93	24		16	9	25	5
Enjoyment of the work itself	27	7	6		6	....	1
The feeling of being creative	21	4	4	8		....	....
Having to give up things I do now because of lower income	15	3	2	1	1		3
The feeling of having something to do with my time	5	1	....	3	....	....	

first that they would miss "The wages," 25 gave as second choice that they would miss most "Having to give up things I do now because of lower income." A further 24 workers indicated as second choice "Being with my friends at work," and 16 chose "Enjoyment of the work itself." These results suggest that the wages they receive and the activities in which they can consequently indulge serve in large measure to shape a worker's views of what his work means to him in relation to his eventual retirement. There is also the suggestion that, despite the fact that the economic aspect is so predominant, many workers acknowledge that the social aspect of work is also important to them.

Eight of the 21 workers who gave first choice to the statement that they would miss most on retirement "The feeling of being creative" ranked second "Enjoyment of the work itself." This indicates that some workers may derive satisfaction from the intrinsic nature of the work situation because it gives them an opportunity to express their creative abilities. It is suggested that among this group of workers are to be found such creative artists as exist in this occupation. However, to substantiate this would require a case study of the individuals who responded in this manner.

b) The ranking of statements by age and marital status.—To determine what variations occurred by age and marital status, the results were arranged according to the rankings given to each statement by the married and single workers in each age group. These rankings are also shown in Table 22.

When workers view their work in relation to their eventual retirement, the economic aspect is most commonly accorded recognition, regardless of their age and marital status. However, the secondary ranking of the statements dealing with those things which workers will miss most when they retire appear to be affected only slightly by these variables. Thus, the results lend some support to the hypothesis that the meanings of work vary according to the age and marital status of individuals within a given skill level.

For example, married and single workers of all ages gave the greatest number of first choices to "The wages." Married workers under 45 years of age gave the second largest number of first choices to "Enjoyment of the work itself" and "Being with my friends at work." Married workers 55–59 years of age gave the second largest number of first choices to "Being with my friends at work." Married workers 60–64 years of age gave their second largest number of first choices to "Enjoyment of the work itself." The single workers under 55 years of age gave the second largest number of first choices to "Being with my friends at work." The few single workers 55–65 years of age gave an equal number of first choices to "The wages" and "Being with my friends at work." It would appear that age has no discernible affect on the listing of things which they would expect to miss most on retirement. Persons of all ages said they would miss "The wages" and "Being with my friends at work." However, the married workers also added "Enjoyment of the work itself."

It is suggested that it may prove profitable to investigate the tentative ordering of the meanings that work has for workers when it is viewed in relation to retirement. Are the same factors which produced the apparent ordering of the meanings of work in the previous section operating to produce the present ordering? How does the particular social situation affect the predominant meaning assigned to work?

VII

The Meanings of Work for
Older Physicians

IN THIS chapter we report on the work and retirement experience of a group of physicians all of whom are over 65 years of age. These men differ in background, training, and work experience from any of the other groups studied in this series.

Physicians are professional men. To be a member of the "professions" in the United States connotes specialized training, higher social status, and middle-class standards of work and leisure. The professional man is expected by his colleagues and clients to keep up with the trends in his occupation as long as he is working. This means that ideally he is always learning new things on the job or in specialized training centers. The professional man is expected, because of his place in the community, to contribute time and money to community endeavors. Thus, he develops a role in community life. The professional man is also expected to be financially able to retire and to maintain his living standards in retirement.

The group reported on here are 138 doctors, 65 years of age or more, all of whom in August, 1949, were members of the American Medical Association, living in Cook County, Illinois. These 138 men were those doctors of a random sample of 427 physicians in this category who completed the schedule *Your Activities and Attitudes*,[1] early in 1950.[2] Thirty-nine older physi-

1. Ruth S. Cavan, Ernest W. Burgess, and Robert J. Havighurst, *Your Activities and Attitudes* (Chicago: Science Research Associates, 1948).

2. The respondent group of 138 doctors has been compared with the total sample of physicians (427). Based on various tests and investigations, we may say that the group of 138 appears to be slightly older than the total sample; a higher proportion of respondents than of nonrespondents in this age group

cians were also interviewed, and the conclusions reported here on the meanings of work are taken from these interviews.

THE MEDICAL PROFESSION

The strong identification of these doctors with the profession of medicine is especially apparent in the interviews. There were several themes which the doctors stressed. These included the growth in their lifetime of medical specialties, the increase in the size of medical fees, the development of the new "wonder" drugs, and the practice of medicine as "dedication." A theme to which the doctors returned again and again was that they represented an early era in the medical profession. Sometimes, these men referred to the days of their youth as "better times," not for themselves particularly, but for medicine.

Within their lifetimes these men had seen great strides in the professionalization of medicine. Within their working lives the discipline had become markedly more scientific, the training of students had been elaborated and standardized, and, most important of all, since 1900 there had been a tremendous growth in medical specialties. Some of these doctors said that both the growth of specialization and the increase in medical fees were factors operating to destroy the "dedication" of the physician.

Dr. Herrick in his *Memories of Eighty Years,* in which he looks back at sixty years of medical practice, expresses the dilemma which confronted certain of the respondents. Of his function as a specialist, Dr. Herrick says: "Yet I had to admit that, no matter how hard I tried, it was impossible to keep pace with the rapid strides made by medicine and cognate sciences. Much of the newer knowledge, so enormous in its mass, eluded me. There was some comfort in knowing that other physicians were in the same predicament."[3]

---

were specialists rather than general practitioners, and a higher proportion of respondents than nonrespondents were still engaged in active practice. In general, the men in the study group differ from other doctors in this age group in that the former were those men most likely to be concerned with medicine as a profession and a way of life. For further details of this study see Dolores Colen Gruen, "The Personal Adjustment of Older Physicians" (unpublished Ph.D. dissertation, University of Chicago Library, 1952).

3. James B. Herrick, *Memories of Eighty Years* (Chicago: University of Chicago Press, 1949), p. 50.

Of medical fees he says: "During my sixty years of practice a marked change has taken place in the matter of fees charged for medical services. In 1889 the ordinary family doctor asked one dollar of the patient who came to his office. A visit at the patient's home was two dollars."[4]

THE MEANINGS OF WORK

The subject of the meaning of work was explored in the interviews which were held with 39 older physicians. Eighteen of the physicians interviewed had filled out and returned the questionnaires, and 21 had not. An effort was made to secure a representative sample of the total group by age and area of residence. Lists were drawn up by area of residence, and telephone calls were made in each area until an appointment was arranged. Thus the interview sample is in some respects more representative of the total group of physicians over 65 than is the sample of those who returned the questionnaire.

Since the interviews covered a variety of subjects, the meaning of work was not explored as thoroughly as it was in studies of the other occupational groups. This should be kept in mind in comparing these results with those of the other groups. Nevertheless, all the meanings found in the other groups emerged from the interviews with physicians, though fewer meanings were mentioned by the average physician than by the average salesperson in the department store, where the person was encouraged to talk at some length about the values of his work.

SERVICE—"FIRST IS GOD, THEN THE DOCTOR, THEN THE PRIEST"

Of the various meanings of work, the physicians most usually recognized and expressed those meanings related to the role of work as being a service to others. Over and over again, they stressed the unique role of the doctor. One of the physicians interviewed described this conception of the doctor's place as, "First is God, then the doctor, then the priest."

A substantial group of doctors spoke of the service aspect of their work as though it was a calling allied to the ministry. They thought of themselves as counselors and comforters.

4. *Ibid.*, p. 156.

Dr. D., a general practitioner, was almost completely retired because of illness. He said that his motivations for going into medicine came from his deep religious feelings. He had attended a religious college and had become very much interested in helping people. He felt that as a doctor he would have a unique position of trust. He talked to a great extent of the doctor's special ability to help in emotional crises. He summed up his position by stating, "A doctor is sort of an oracle. He sees beneath the front that people put up." He felt that because of his place in the community, helping humanity should be foremost to a doctor; it even should take precedence over his medical skill.

Another physician told of entering the medical field from a religious motivation. He, too, expressed the feeling that a good deal of a doctor's helpfulness came from emotional therapy that he was in the position to administer.

Dr. B., a general practitioner in active practice, said that the field of medicine was his second choice. He had really wanted to be a priest but felt that he had too many frailties. He talked about how he was able to help a good many of his patients through advice. He said that he took a very authoritative role with his patients so that his advice had some weight. Sometimes his help didn't come through actual medical facility but through words and soda pills. He felt that he was able to do this because of the unique position that he held in his patients' lives.

Many doctors expressed the feeling that their real help to their patients came from their personal skill as individuals dealing with individuals rather than the application of medical knowledge. This giving of one's self was described as being very taxing and demanding. Some doctors seemed to enjoy this aspect of their practice tremendously. They expressed the feeling that their effectiveness depends on this personal give and take.

Dr. M. stated: "There is something wonderful about having people depend upon you, have trust in you. . . . It is very important for the doctor to get the feeling that the patient needs and trusts him. When this confidence is had, the field of medicine is a nice profession to grow old in because one mellows with time."

As a doctor approaches the end of his work, he sometimes becomes quite dependent on the assurance his patients give him that he has helped them. Dr. M. is a specialist in diseases of the eye, ear, nose, and throat. The interviewer waited to see him until he had finished with a patient.

As the patient went out, she asked when she should phone him. Dr. M. replied, "Oh, call me tomorrow." The doctor mentioned this when he described the meaning of work to him. He said, "What do I get out of my practice? It's hard to tell. I guess it's helping people. I enjoy the feeling that I'm needed. I should have told that lady to call me the day after tomorrow, but I'd like to hear tomorrow how she's getting along. I'm just conceited enough to think that I helped her."

In addition to saying that their work enabled them to be of service to others, some doctors coupled this statement with remarks that indicated they secured self-respect and recognition from others, as is seen in the following excerpts.

From all outward appearances, Dr. G. was no longer practicing. He rented two rooms of a four-room cold-water flat over a grocery store. The other two rooms were occupied by a Negro family of four. Dr. G's rooms were very messy and obviously not set up for professional work. There was no sign anywhere on the premises indicating that he was a doctor.

Dr. G. said that he had received his medical training in Germany, his homeland. He came to the United States at the beginning of this century. He had been practicing in his present neighborhood for most of forty years. At the present time he was still caring for some of his old patients and visited patients for the city welfare department for a dollar a call. He showed the interviewer a stack of what looked like old checkbooks. The doctor said proudly, "These are my babies." It appeared that these were birth-certificate stubs of the babies he had delivered.

When asked about retirement, Dr. G. stated: "A doctor is like a minister. He can't retire. What'll I do if a patient comes to me with a cut hand? Shall I say, 'Oh, no, you can't come to me with a cut hand. I'm retired.' No, a doctor can't retire. A doctor's job is always to be with his patients."

While Dr. G.'s living conditions are somewhat unusual, his feelings are those of most of the physicians interviewed. A more unusual picture is presented by Dr. L.

Dr. L., a specialist in diseases of the eye, carried on his practice from nine to five every day at his office. He said that he is pretty much alone in the world since his wife died.

He wants to continue working. A few years ago he had suffered from an attack of tuberculosis, which he had had as a young man. He was away from his office for some time and thought of retiring. Dr. L. belongs to a fraternal order which has a home for its aged members. He went there to visit and talked to the administration about the possibility of going there to live and carrying on some medical work. They told him that if he were to go there he would have to forget that he ever was a doctor and become an ordinary inmate. Dr. L. thought it over carefully and decided that he just couldn't give up his identity as a doctor. He would deteriorate if he ever did that. He said, "One thing that my work gives me is contact with people. There's something wonderful about having people depend upon you, having trust in you." Dr. L. compared the doctor to a father-confessor in that they both have the opportunity really to know people. Following this thought, he said that the young doctors were making a mistake by charging high fees. Dr. L. stated that he felt that a doctor must sell himself, not his services, to the patient, and that it is very important for the doctor to get the feeling that the patient needs and trusts him.

WORK MEANS PRESTIGE—"YOU CAN GET IN BY JUST SENDING YOUR CARD"

A second meaning of work mentioned by the physicians is that work is a source of prestige. Some doctors stated that to be a physician meant that one belonged to an elite class. It meant that one associated with important people and was in a position of leadership in the community.

This feeling was expressed by Dr. I., who described his work as . . . "a nice clean profession. It has prestige and you can get into so many inaccessable places just by sending in your card." Dr. I. told of the time that he wanted to visit someone who was in jail. The attendant told him that he could not possibly get in. He just gave the attendant his card and the latter said with reverence, "Oh, come in, doctor."

WORK MEANS SELF-EXPRESSION—"WORK MEANS FULFILMENT OF SELF"

A third meaning of work for physicians is that work is a form of creativity or a means of self-expression. For many physicians the practice of medicine is a means by which they made their impression on life. It gives them a sense of being creative, of functioning as a whole rather than as a segmental person. One doctor, a psychiatrist, described the situation as follows:

Dr. J. said that he was only able to be partially active at the present time. He stated that he enjoyed doing some work even if he could not work full time. He went on to say that he felt that the trouble with some people is that they give work a negative connotation. They talk about play as though it were something positive, and about work as something negative. Dr. J. felt that people should realize that work meant "fulfilment of self." He pointed out that only through work could a person find co-ordination of mind and body.

A somewhat comparable feeling was reported by Dr. B., age 82.

When asked what work had meant to him, Dr. B. answered simply, "I enjoyed it." He elaborated by saying that he enjoyed people and enjoyed the mental stimulation that his work gave him. He said before he had had the several coronary attacks which had somewhat incapacitated him, he used to teach in the morning, carry on a clinic, work during the day in his office, and take home calls. Many times when he finally reached his own home in the evening he would use his leisure for writing technical or learned articles.

WORK MEANS ROUTINE—"I HAVE ENOUGH MONEY TO RETIRE, BUT DON'T KNOW WHAT I WOULD DO"

Work is a form of routine activity. It fills the day and gives body to life, as was said in one way or another by several men. Indeed, some physicians stated that work was necessary for their well-being. They expressed fears that without work they would grow "rusty" and feel "as though they were put on the shelf," and indeed some doctors stated that should they stop work they would probably die shortly.

The reslessness which one physician felt because of curtailed activity is indicated in the following excerpt:

Dr. N. maintains a very clean, orderly office in a suburban business district. One is at once impressed with the restlessness of this man. His step is brisk, perhaps a little too brisk. His words are short and clipped. His face is always flushed, as though he was never in repose.

After inviting the interviewer into his office, Dr. N. sat down at his desk for the interview. Throughout the interview he fingered one object or another. He had two pairs of glasses which he would change intermittently. Several times he threw a pencil across his desk as he made a point.

Dr. N. said that he gave up his regular practice a few years before because of illness. However, he managed to retain a limited office practice. He works mainly with some of his old patients. He keeps office hours six days a week from one to three and seven to eight. He said that he didn't know what he would do were he to give up work. He stated that he is even restless on his day off.

One reason he gave for continuing working was because of some advice he had given his father, also a physician. When his father reached 69, Dr. N. told him that he should retire. Ten years later, his father told Dr. N. that this was the worst advice that he had ever given him. His father said that because of retirement he had lost his independence. He couldn't even walk out of the house without someone asking him where he was going.

As for himself, Dr. N. stated, "Life is very lonesome. We have no children. I used to have a lot of hobbies, such as golf, hunting, fishing, and billiards, but I can't even do them any more. I really didn't know how to play even when I was active. I used to be called away from the golf course three out of ten times. So, I really don't know what to do with my time."

For Dr. N., then, the primary meaning of work is a means of filling time, with the secondary meaning that it enables him to keep active and independent. Similarly, Dr. S. points out that if he did not work he would not know how to fill his day.

Dr. S. is a widower. He makes his home now with his son and daughter-in-law and their children. Dr. S. maintains a nine-to-five working schedule and limits all his work to his office. He breaks up this routine by lengthy yearly vacations. Dr. S. does not believe that this harms his practice, since he always has an office full of patients waiting for him the day he comes back from one of his trips.

When asked why he continued working, Dr. S. said, "I have enough money to retire, but I don't know what I would do. There are only two things that I know, and these are farming and medicine. I have been practicing medicine so long that I don't think I would like farming again."

WORK MEANS ECONOMIC GAIN—"THE MONEY"

For some few physicians the economic gain secured from their practice was the most important part of work to them. This was brought out clearly in the interview with Dr. D.

Dr. D. is both a practicing dentist and a physician. He had been a dentist first but continued teaching in a newly created dental school until he got his M.D. degree. He said that this arrangement has worked out very well for him, as he has most of his patients for both medical and dental treatment.

Dr. D. said that his earliest ambition was to be a printer. He had served some of his apprenticeship as a printer when he decided to take up medicine. He said that he has always been happy that he did this, since "I have been able to do very well."

Dr. D. talked at some length about how a doctor had to be careful to "steer clear" of patients who would or could not pay their bills. He told a story about how he once took care of a leukemia patient. It was necessary for him to see her very often, sometimes every day. He saw that the family of the patient was assuming a greater financial burden than they could afford. So he convinced the patient's mother that she should take the daughter to another city. He said, "I don't know how they got her down there, but, do you know, that girl lived for nine months more. I never would have gotten that bill paid. I still haven't gotten it paid. Look how much more they would have owed me."

When asked what he felt he had gotten most from the practice of medicine, Dr. D. laughed and jingled some change in his pocket and said, "The money."

To those few physicians who put the economic meaning of their practice first, money pervaded their conversation and seemed most important in every topic they discussed. The following excerpt from an interview with Dr. O. is interesting because of a slip that the doctor made in describing his practice.

Dr. O. had spent most of his career in medical education. He had been active head of a medical department for years while maintaining a specialty practice with his son. When he retired from teaching, he turned his efforts to his practice.

He said that quitting his former work was somewhat of a relief. He had not been well, and his work had become demanding. Now he was able to work whenever he felt like it. The financial rewards were very good. He became quite enthusiastic at this point. He spoke of his practice as "a growing business." He caught himself and qualified this phrase by talking of the "extensive practice." He seemed a little embarrassed by this slip.

IT'S NICE WORK

Almost a unique attitude comes out in conversation with older physicians about their jobs. In a variety of ways they seem to be saying, "It's nice work." The reasons for the doctor's calling being "nice work" cluster around the ideas of prestige, income, independence, and interest. When work gives all these things to a man, why should he give it up?

Dr. R. described his routine of being from nine to five in the office. He said that he likes medicine and that he likes to work with people. He added that his work was now a family enterprise. A few years ago he dismissed his nurse, and his wife came to take the nurse's place. After raising three children, his wife decided that she would enjoy working along with him. They are able to work steadily but not too hard. On week ends they go to their cottage at the dunes. He said that they both enjoy this arrangement.

Another physician, who was able to maintain a practice commensurate with his needs and capacities, expressed satisfaction with his work.

Dr. E., who limits his general practice work to his office, said, "I like the work. It's a wonderful field to grow old in. Why, I had a patient in this morning. He's 62, but he's older than his years. He works in a drafty elevator. He has three years to go for Social Security, and then what has he got? I can work here as much as I want. I'm my own boss."

Only rarely did a doctor make complaints, and then it was usually about the ingratitude of patients.

Dr. S. said that he had started off with an idealistic point of view. Then he found that people do not appreciate idealism. He said that he had become disappointed in trying to help them. People thought nothing of calling him up at two or three o'clock in the morning and then not paying their bill. He said that one reason that he did not take night calls any more was that the ones who called him to their homes were the last ones to pay. He told of the man who had called him at three o'clock in the morning to come over to see his wife. The doctor sent the bill month after month. The man never paid. So one morning at three o'clock Dr. S. got on the phone and called the man. The man was very angry. Dr. S. said, "I'm going to do it tonight, and I'm going to do it every night I come in late until you pay the bill." He stressed that even though you wanted to help people, you couldn't show them that you wanted to help them. You couldn't let them tramp on you, because they would if they had the chance.

RANKING THE MEANINGS OF WORK

The doctors themselves were not asked to rank the various possible meanings that work had for their lives. They were simply encouraged to say what work had meant to them. Consequently some spoke more explicitly than others did about the meaning of their work, and some mentioned several meanings, while others did not express themselves clearly enough on this subject to permit inferring a particular meaning from what they said. With these reservations concerning the procedure used, we may report the result of coding the interviews for the various meanings of work. The data are presented in Table 24. The most frequent meaning mentioned was that of service to people, which was usually tied to the idea that this work made the doctor a unique and socially valuable person. Thirty-eight per cent of the physicians spoke of this meaning of their work.

The next meaning in order of frequency was association, men-

TABLE 24

MEANINGS IN THEIR WORK AS REPORTED BY
39 PHYSICIANS, 65 AND OVER

Meaning	No. Re- porting This Meaning	Percentage of Physicians Who Iden- tified This Meaning
1. Money	3	8
2. Routine	7	18
3, *a*. Self-respect	3	8
3, *b*. Prestige, recognition from others	6	15
4. Association, friendship	9	23
5, *a*, *b*, and *c*. Creativity, self-expression	7	18
5, *d*. Service to others	15	38

tioned by 23 per cent of the men. In this connection the doctor usually spoke of liking to work with people. It was not so much that he felt he was associating with his friends as that he liked to work with people rather than with things.

Three meanings come next, with 15–18 per cent of the replies. Work as a source of self-expression, creativity, or intrinsic enjoyment was one of these. Probably this was taken for granted by many, since only one or two expressed any feeling of unpleasantness or burdensomeness about their work. An equal number of doctors mentioned their work as a pleasant routine, a way of making the time pass. Fifteen per cent spoke of their work as a source of prestige or the respect of others.

Only 8 per cent made any point of mentioning the money they made as an important meaning of their work. Many took this for granted, while a very few told of their present economic insecurity and said that they were practicing from economic necessity.

From the questionnaire study of doctors aged 65 years or over, our schedule and interview materials indicate that, except on rare occasions, physicians do not retire while they are in reasonably good physical condition.

Ninety-three of the 138 respondents were still working either full or part time. A closer examination of what constituted full-time activities for the older doctor was made for the interview group of 39 cases. Of those physicians who were working full time, only four men said that their program of full-time activities at the time of the interview was similar to the program which they had followed at the height of their practice. Most of the men who were working full time described their practice as being different from what it used to be. Although they worked a full day, they had reduced activities which had become too difficult for them. Activities eliminated included the making of home calls and night visits and the practice of obstetrics and surgery.

The amount of work activity varied with the age of the physician. The majority of the physicians in the age group 65–75 appeared to be engaged in some type of work, and there were even a few doctors who continued to be active in the profession beyond this age. Other men, although working full time, had reduced their tasks and responsibilities by acquiring assistants.

The doctors gave a variety of reasons for decreasing their activities. The single most important reason was the awareness of fatigue. Frequently the decision to change the nature of practice followed a sudden illness such as heart disease.

But even when his physical capacity was obvious and burdening, the doctor tended to hold to his identity as an active member of his profession.

A case in point is Dr. C. The doctor was sitting in a wheelchair with a robe draped over his legs. He was wearing an old sweater. It was brought out later that he had suffered a stroke a few years before and now was in treatment for cataracts.

During most of the interview the doctor spoke as though he were actively engaged in his work. His wife mentioned his recent illnesses, frequently telling about the difficulties they had had getting suitable medical attention from the younger doctors. Dr. C. did not seem to want to dwell on this topic. He went into an elaborate discourse about his former practice, discussing some cases in detail. He talked of how some of his earliest patients would still visit him. He also mentioned several of his medical discoveries and how he had played an important part in the sanitation of the city's water supply. He talked as if his work were temporarily suspended because of his illness but not over.

While most of the doctors refused to retire until illness or fatigue forced them to do so, a small number were retired while active and healthy, and they had a different attitude toward retirement as well as toward their profession. For them the work as a physician seemed to be only one of several areas of self-expression. As they reached later maturity, they became more active in their other fields and less concerned with the practice of medicine.

Dr. D. seemed to be more interested in some type of social work than he was in medicine.

He said that he had entered the field of medicine because he felt that therein he could best serve mankind. He had thought about being a teacher or a minister but felt that his shyness would handicap him from being effective. His main interest was in helping people. He married a social worker, and they both became interested in the missionary movement. Several times he was called upon to give up his practice to engage in missionary work in Africa. He served the movement as a headmaster in a school. After coming back from his last assignment, he decided to settle down. He moved to a suburb because he was interested in their school system. He became very active in the P.T.A. group of the school his children attended. He also maintained active contact with his undergraduate institution. He served on the board of trustees. As he put it, "I found that I could not devote time to both my medical practice and my educational interests, so I began to refer my patients to my brother and nephew. My retirement was accomplished by my patients without my making a decision. But I was never sorry." At the present time Dr. D. is very active in a Borrowed Time club.

In many ways, Dr. T.'s retirement followed a similar pattern. He, too, was a man with a multitude of interests. Retirement to him meant dropping his work activities and increasing his interest in other fields.

Dr. T. still kept an office, but, as he had told the interviewer on the phone, it had no semblance to an active physician's office. The place was strewn with old papers and magazines. When the interviewer arrived, the doctor was busily engaged in wrapping several large cartons. He said that they were much-needed foodstuffs for friends and relatives in Britain.

Dr. T. told the interviewer that he had retired from work activity six years before (at the age of 80). He had accomplished his retirement by taking the gold lettering off his window. He said that he hadn't sent out a bill since that time. While some of his old patients would still ask him to give them a check-up, he has considered it as a deed of friendship rather than as a professional visit.

He said that he spends his time with his many interests and hobbies. Some of his hobbies have undergone change with the years, such as his former love of mountain-climbing and hiking. He showed the interviewer some of the pictures taken on his sojourns.

Cutting and polishing precious stones was a hobby that he had maintained through a lifetime. He has lectured to many lay and art groups in this field.

The interviewer got an impression of Dr. T.'s extreme interest in people. He said that at the present time he spends a lot of time with people. It seemed that Dr. T.'s energies had not been consumed in medical practice.

These examples show that retirement comes more easily to people who have found many satisfactions outside of their lifework, apparently only a small proportion of men in the profession of medicine.

For the physicians in our study, with very few exceptions, to be a doctor was to be doing the best of all possible jobs in the best of all possible professions. In the main, the physicians realized that work had some special meaning to them, and almost all of them felt that not to work would be seriously harmful psychologically, if not physically; as long as they were physically able, they continued as "doctors," either in full-time practice alone or with an assistant or as part-time practitioners or specialists.

VIII

A Comparison of the Meanings of Work and Retirement among Different Occupational Groups

FROM our studies of the meanings of work to members of five occupational groups, what can we conclude about the differences between occupational groups and what can we say about the significance of retirement in their lives? We planned the series of studies with the following hypotheses in mind.

1. Workers at the lower skill and socioeconomic levels regard their work more frequently as merely a way to earn a living and in general recognize fewer extra-financial meanings in their work than do workers of higher skill and socioeconomic levels.

2. Workers who regard work primarily in terms of its financial meaning will be more favorable toward retirement at age 65 than workers who experience more extra-financial meanings in their work.

3. Those persons who stress meanings of work other than those of earning a living will prefer to continue working past 65.

Since the detailed methods of the studies in this series varied somewhat, it is difficult to make a clear-cut test of these hypotheses in so far as they involve comparison of occupational groups. As we have already noted, the exploratory nature of these studies made it desirable to modify each study as it came along in the light of previous experience, and consequently no two studies asked precisely the same questions about meanings of work and retirement or analyzed the data in precisely the same categories.

Nevertheless, the studies were enough alike in design and interpretation of data to permit comparison of results and a cautious kind of generalization.[1]

THE MEANINGS OF WORK

In all the groups studied work was found to have meanings in addition to that of earning a living. Tables 25 and 26 represent two ways of comparing the frequencies with which the various values of work are mentioned by the several occupational groups. These tables are both unsatisfactory for careful comparisons, but they are the best we could do in the face of the differences among the several studies.

Table 25 reports the percentages of people in the five occupational groups who mentioned the various meanings of work. This table is the most accurate way of summarizing our data on the meanings of work, but it also indicates the difficulties that lie in the way of making comparisons. For one thing, the categories of analysis are not identical in all the studies. "Service to others" was used as a category explicitly in two groups and implicitly in another ("Work has given me a chance to be useful") but not at all in three groups. The distribution of other responses is affected by the presence or absence of the "service" category. If it was mentioned by a respondent, but not allowed for as a specific category, it probably was placed in one of the other categories and thus served to increase the frequencies in them. "Routine" was not offered as a possible choice to the skilled craftsmen aged below 65 on their questionnaire, and therefore some who would have indicated this were led to choose other meanings instead.

1. A note about the statistical significance of these findings is appropriate at this point. The steelworker and coal-miner studies were based upon a random sample of a larger population. The random sample of skilled craftsmen under the age of 65 produced only a 47 per cent response, and no attempt to generalize beyond the respondents was made. The study of skilled craftsmen 65 years and older was based upon a complete universe. The salesclerk study was based upon a complete universe of male clerks and a stratified random sample of women to match the male group. The study of physicians was not made upon a random sample. Thus, it would appear that rigorous statistical cross-comparisons cannot be made. The discussions of this chapter, therefore, are limited mainly to a qualitative comparison of the groups and a rather cautious attempt at presenting trends which the researchers felt to be meaningful but for which limits of error could not be calculated.

Furthermore, the technique used in the study of salespeople encouraged them to talk about as many meanings of work as possible, while that employed with the coal-miners limited them to one meaning apiece, and the other studies fell between these two extremes.

TABLE 25

PERCENTAGE FREQUENCY OF MENTION OF THE VARIOUS MEANINGS
OF WORK FOR THE FIVE OCCUPATIONAL GROUPS

MEANING	STEELWORK- ERS (UN- SKILLED AND SEMI- SKILLED)	COAL- MINERS	SKILLED CRAFTSMEN		SALES- PEOPLE	PHYSICIANS
			20–64	Over 65		
1. Money............	100	86	29*	84	†	8
2. Routine..........	34	19	‡	31	89	18
3, *a.* Self-respect.....	19(3, *a, b*)	18(3, *a, b*)	49	50(3, *a, b*)	49	8
3, *b.* Prestige, respect of others............	....	....	24	....	45	15
4. Association........	18	19	30	40	85	23
5, *a.* Purposeful activ- ity..............	10	11(5, *a, c*)	....	....	61	....
5, *b.* Creativity, self- expression, intrinsic enjoyment........	5	‡	28	35	47	18(5, *a, b, c*)
5, *c.* New experience..	1	....	18	27	‡	....
5, *d.* Service to others.	‡	16§	‡	‡	41	38
No meaning other than that of earning a liv- ing..............	34	18	16	22	0	0
No. of people respond- ing..............	128	153	242	208	74	39

* "My work has been *only* a way of earning a living."
† Assumed that this was present for all.
‡ Not covered in the questionnaire or interview.
§ "Work has given me a chance to be useful."

Perhaps a more useful way of comparing the several occupational groups is represented in Table 26, where the relative frequency of mention of the various meanings is obtained by assuming each group to have been limited to one response per person and further assuming that the relative frequencies of the various meanings within the group would be unchanged from the results of Table 25 by this procedure. In other words, the frequencies of Table 25 are converted to relative numbers on the assumption that each group gave 100 responses. This makes no change in the results for coal-miners and makes a maximum change in the figures for salespeople. The latter figures are therefore the most open to error because of this procedure.

Table 26 has the advantage of facilitating comparisons between the several occupational groups. It shows the following things:

1. The workers of lower skill and socioeconomic status are more likely to see their work as having no other meaning than that of earning money.

TABLE 26

COMPARISON OF THE FIVE OCCUPATIONAL GROUPS
ON THE MEANINGS OF WORK

(Relative Percentages Assuming Each Group To
Have Given One Response per Person)

MEANING	STEELWORKERS (UNSKILLED AND SEMI-SKILLED)	COAL-MINERS	SKILLED CRAFTSMEN		SALES-PEOPLE	PHYSICIANS
			20–64	Over 65		
1. No meaning other than money	28	18	10	11	0	0
2. Routine	28	19	*	15	21	15
3, *a.* Self-respect	....	....	30	....	12	7
3, *b.* Prestige, respect of others	16(3, *a*, *b*)	18(3, *a*, *b*)	15	24(3, *a*, *b*)	11	13
4. Association	15	19	18	20	20	19
5, *a, b, c.* Purposeful activity, self-expression, new experience	13	11	28	30	26	15
5, *d.* Service to others	*	16†	*	*	10	32
No. of people responding	128	153	242	208	74	39

* Not covered in the questionnaire or interview.
† "Work has given me a chance to be useful."

2. The five occupational groups all value "association" about equally as a meaning of work.

3. Work as a routine which makes the time pass is recognized about equally by all five groups.

4. All groups discover self-respect and secure respect or recognition from others by means of their work, and there is probably no reliable difference among them in the prevalence

of this meaning. While it seems to be highest among the skilled craftsmen, this may have resulted from the fact that the category "Service to others" was not used in that particular study, and anyone to whom this meaning was especially significant may have mentioned self-respect or the respect of others which he obtained as a result of the service element in his work.

5. The physicians show a high awareness of the "Service to others" meaning in their work. This may be characteristic of the "service" professions.

6. Work is important as a source of interesting, purposeful activity and as a source of intrinsic enjoyment for all five groups, but there may be reliable differences between them in this respect.

The skilled craft and white-collar groups stressed the extra-financial meanings of work to a much greater extent than did the workers in heavy industry, thus bearing out our hypothesis that these meanings of work become more and more important as we ascend the occupational and skill ladders. However, it is not only the extent to which these meanings were stressed but also the patterns in which they occurred that reveal the nature of work experience.

Steelworkers and Coal-Miners

Among these two groups employed at perhaps some of the least desirable jobs which an industrial society has to offer, we find the strongest emphasis placed on work as only a way of earning a living. It is not surprising that a lifetime spent at what once were among society's most burdensome and lowest-paid jobs—ones at which most men worked as a matter of necessity rather than choice—should reveal few work satisfactions. Yet we did find that, even at this occupational level, the job had come to play certain very definite parts in the life of many persons. Two-thirds of the steelworker group and four-fifths[2] of

2. Although a smaller percentage of coal-miners indicated that work was only a way of earning a living than did steelworkers, this difference can probably be attributed to the interview technique. In the coal-miner study, interviewers read off a list of work meanings to the subject, and, where earning a living was selected first, the subject was asked to indicate another meaning as well. This was the only group where the interviewer actually pressed the

the coal-miners indicated that earning a living was not the only meaning which work has had for them.

There was a great deal of similarity in the meanings observed and their frequency of occurrence in both groups, particularly when they are contrasted with the skilled craft and white-collar groups. To this extent we have a "pattern" of meanings which might be considered typical of lower-skilled workers in heavy industry.

Both groups resembled each other in the extent to which work as association and a source of self-respect was stressed and in the nature of their meaning for each. Association meant mostly "being with the gang" in both cases. Self-respect and the respect of others seemed to refer to the sense of personal worth and status which their particular job gave them among other members of their work group and in their families. There was little indication in either group that self-respect was based on a "prestigeful occupation," that is, one which gave them a desirable status in the larger society.

Work as a routine also had a peculiar intensity of meaning for members of both groups. Work was a burdensome and even dangerous task for these men, yet it was a familiar routine around which life as they knew it seemed to revolve. It received its strongest emphasis among the steelworker group, where many seemed to regard the routine of work as the routine of life and reasoned that if work stopped so would life itself.

Perhaps the greatest difference observed among the two groups was in the category of work meanings classified as "meaningful life-experience," and even here the difference was not a large one. Meaningful life-experience refers to work as an intellectual experience—one which presents a problem and challenges the individual to solve it, which provides the stimulus of new situations, new ideas, new experience, and which enables him to evaluate the routine of work in terms of such concepts

---

subject for extra-economic meanings. It is probably significant that under these conditions 18 per cent of the miners would admit no other meaning than that of earning a living. For coal-miners we believe that interview procedures similar to those of the steelworker study would produce a percentage of "earning a living only" responses in the 30 per cent range as was found among the steelworkers.

as purpose, achievement, responsibility, and usefulness. Although work as an intellectual experience was not an important aspect of the work experience of these two groups when contrasted with the skilled craftsmen or white-collar sales group studied, still we find that work seemed to offer a somewhat greater challenge for the coal-miner than it did for the steelworker.

There was little of the craftsmen's sense of achievement in either coal-mining or steel work at these skill levels; that is, there was not the challenge of the product to be designed, executed, and carried through to its completion. These men had a transient relation to their product. They performed a single and usually repetitive operation on it one step along its way, without seeing its beginning or end. (This is possibly somewhat less true of coal-miners than steelworkers.) The challenge of their jobs, then, was the challenge of the tool or operation to be mastered, of the production record to be equaled or beaten, or of the environment to be conquered. But only a few of the operations in coal-mining or steelworking yielded any sense of achievement to the operators; also very few men in either group seemed to regard the matching of a production record as a personal challenge. It was primarily in the challenge of their environment that their work experience differed. The coal-miners had a very personal sense of being pitted against their environment and expressed feelings of accomplishment and pride at having conquered it. Their work literally takes them from the face of the earth down into a strange and terrible world where the danger of accident, explosion, and death is always present. The danger is both a personalized and a dramatic one—the work gang is pitted against the mine. Victory is dependent upon each man's holding up his end. Victory is not only the sense of having cheated death (which comes out very strongly in the interview material); it is also the sense of having achieved life through one's own efforts and those of one's fellow-workers.

Skilled Craftsmen and Salesclerks

The skilled craftsmen studied are characterized by a very high degree of emphasis on work as a source of self-respect and the respect of others, a moderate degree of emphasis on the meaningful life-experience and association of their jobs, and a relatively low degree of emphasis on work as a routine activity. Self-respect here refers to the status accorded to a skilled craftsman in the community as well as the recognition obtained in the work group and the family. The job was apparently one of their own choosing for many of them—one which they would choose again if they could live their lives over again and which they would strongly recommend to a young man today. It is regarded as one of the more desirable jobs which society has to offer.

About 40 per cent of the group regarded work as a chance to be with and work with others. Association here refers to the fellow-worker relationships which exist on the job itself and also may include relationships with other workers of their craft away from the job as well. Routine is the least important of the meanings associated with working at this skilled trade. There is little in the job itself that requires repetitive automatic action. The routine referred to may also include the habit of being at a fixed place during a fixed set of hours for five days a week and also the habit of making the trip to and from the place of work. But the distinctive character, the flavor of work experience in this skilled craft, is probably reflected in the nature of this work as "meaningful life-experience," which ranked next to self-respect in frequency of occurrence. Here we find revealed the craftsman who commands the respect accorded to the skilled technician in our society and who also experiences the sense of creativity and accomplishment of the artisan in his work. The worker is matched against his materials and by his skill and ingenuity creates a purposeful object out of an inanimate mass.

The salesclerks were perhaps the most verbally fluent of the respondents in this study, and the abundance of meanings which they attached to their work may be, in part, evidence of their fluency. Between 80 and 90 per cent of all the salesclerks interviewed indicated that work had the meaning of routine, association, and meaningful life-experience for them; and about half of the group indicated that work was also a source of self-respect.

Far more than the steelworkers and coal-miners, the sales-clerks are able to state a philosophy of work. Assuming that work is important as a means of earning a living, they do not bother to discuss it in this way but speak readily and fully of the extra-economic meanings of their work. All aspects of work, even routine and association, become "meaningful life-experi-ence."

If there is a philosophy of work for the salesclerk, it is one that is perhaps best summed up by the phrase "the selling game." Work has the implication of being more than a task, more than a way of earning a living with additional meanings which have arisen incidental to its primary purpose. The primary purpose of work (i.e., earning a living) has undergone a subtle change. It has now become "playing the game," and the other aspects of work experience are no longer incidental; they are rationalized in terms of the "game." The completion of the sale, the conquering of the customer, represents the challenge or the "meaningful life-experience" of selling. The researcher is hard pressed to separate out the other meanings of work. Being with people and meeting new people are valued not simply for their own sake, as in the other groups studied, but also because it offers a chance for new conquests in the selling game.

The Physician

The study of the physician provided us with our only glimpse of the work of the professional man. To be a member of the "professions" in the United States gives an added significance to the job. First of all, it implies highly specialized training of an academic or "learned" variety, higher social status, and usual-ly a higher income level. In the case of the physicians all these conditions were met. Second, being a member of the professions denotes a "calling," an occupation which society limits to a specially qualified and trusted few. The exclusiveness of their occupation, in turn, imposes upon its members a sense of public trust or obligation. (The Hippocratic oath of the physician is an example of this public trust.) These conditions can be re-garded as the social "atmosphere" surrounding the practice of a profession in our country. Even the man who in his professional behavior has rejected this sense of public trust or "calling" knows of its existence and may feel obliged to rationalize his conduct accordingly.

It is not surprising, therefore, that all the physicians studied stressed the extra-economic aspects of their jobs. Most of them conceived of their work in terms of the public "service" which they performed. Service would seem to be the *raison d'être* for the medical man; in a sense it was a work motif that was probably common to all the doctors studied. For example, 23 per cent of them regarded association as an outstanding meaning of their job but described this association in terms of their relations with the public they served rather than with their professional colleagues. None of this group of physicians stated that his work was only a way of earning a living.

Similarities among the Groups

Having discussed the five occupational groups with emphasis upon the *different* meanings that work has for them, we may now reverse the point of view and say that certain of the meanings people find in their work are remarkably similar from one occupation to another. For instance, in Table 26 the meaning of association appears with nearly the same relative frequency in such widely diverse occupations as steelmaking and the practice of medicine. Further, differences in the degree to which this meaning was stressed were greater within occupational groups than between them. This seems to suggest that the occurrence of certain meanings of work may be more closely related to such individual factors as personal value hierarchies and particular histories of work experience than it is to the nature of work in any given occupation. However, this could only be true within limits, since a job which required one to work alone most of the time and involved work with materials rather than with people could not give much opportunity for the meaning of "association." Any more accurate comparative statements about the meanings of work in various occupations must wait upon a systematic study of workers in various occupations using the same procedures of analysis of the data for all occupations.

Some indication of what this would bring is given by an extension of Bower's study of salespeople. She also studied two other groups of people working in the department store—workroom personnel and merchandise handlers. The workroom personnel were tailors, seamstresses, and other craftsmen, while the merchandise handlers were employed at the less skilled jobs

TABLE 27

COMPARISON OF THREE GROUPS OF DEPART-
MENT-STORE WORKERS

Meaning	Sales-people	Work-room Personnel	Mer-chandise Handlers
	Percentage of Workers Mentioning the Various Meanings of Work		
2. Routine...............	89	88	89
3, *a*. Self-respect...........	49	34	51
3, *b*. Recognition by others..	45	38	21
4. Association.............	85	50	66
5, *a*. Purposeful activity....	61	47	37
5, *b*. Intrinsic enjoyment....	47	21	9
5, *d*. Service to others......	41	6	6
	Percentage of Workers Who Speak of the Various Meanings as "Highly Important"		
2. Routine...............	35	59	60
3, *a*. Self-respect...........	7	15	6
3, *b*. Recognition by others..	4	....	....
4. Association.............	27	16	9
5, *a*. Purposeful activity....	18	19	11
5, *b*. Intrinsic enjoyment....	....	6	....
5, *d*. Service to others......	....	....	....

of handling, storing, marking, and wrapping merchandise. Bower used the same kind of interview and the same kind of analysis with all three groups.

Table 27 reports the comparison of the three groups. The top half of the table gives the percentages of workers who mentioned the various meanings of work and is thus comparable to Table 25. The three groups are much alike, and the only statistically reliable differences are to be found in work as a means of "association," "service to others," and "intrinsic enjoyment." Furthermore, the salespeople mentioned more meanings of work than did the other two groups, as we should expect on the basis of the previous comparisons with manual workers.

Bower also categorized the responses of the workers in a three-point scale in terms of the importance to them of the meaning mentioned. This kind of analysis resulted in the lower part of Table 27, in which the percentages of people are given who indicated that a particular meaning was "highly important" to them. Here we see two reliable differences. If the workroom personnel and merchandise handlers are combined into a single group so as to get the advantage of larger numbers, we find reliable differences in the meanings of "routine" and "association" only.

POSITIVE AND NEGATIVE VALUES OF WORK—A SUGGESTION FOR FURTHER RESEARCH

During these studies of the meanings of work, it became clear to us that we had oversimplified the matter by limiting our analysis of the meanings of work to the positive side—the positive values or satisfactions that a worker finds in his job. Probably every job has both positive and negative values for the worker. If the positive values are great enough, the job makes a major contribution to the satisfactions which the worker gets from life. For example, an artist who recognizes his work both as a way of earning a living and as an opportunity for creative self-expression may be well satisfied if he gets some of both values, while another artist who has a very profitable commercial business may be less happy because he discovers so little of intrinsic pleasure in his work. The fortunate person is one who gets substantial satisfaction from one or more of the positive values and finds little negative value in his work.

One reason that unskilled workers are more ready to retire if they have economic security than are workers with higher skill is probably that the unskilled workers find more negative values in their work than do those higher on the economic scale. For instance, certain steelworkers who recognized that their work gave them a routine to live by and thus structured their lives also tended to find dissatisfaction in this routine because it was exhausting and dangerous, while salespeople, who recognized the same meaning of routine in their work, found satisfaction in the routine because it was relative pleasant and interesting.

It should be possible in a study of meanings of work to investigate the degree of positive or negative value attached to each meaning which a person experiences. Table 28 illustrates this kind of design for a research.

TABLE 28

POSITIVE AND NEGATIVE VALUES OF WORK

Positive	Negative
1. Provides good living	Pay is inadequate
2. Fills the day comfortably; makes time pass quickly; a pleasant routine	Dull, boring; or exhausting, dangerous
3, *a*. Brings self-respect	Reduces self-respect
3, *b*. Brings prestige; recognition from others	Low status: no prestige
4. Provides association with nice people; friendship	Forces association with people one does not like
5, *a*. Provides interesting experience; purposeful activity	Uninteresting
5, *b*. Intrinsic enjoyment; self-expression, creativity	Distasteful
5, *d*. Permits service to others	No opportunity for service

By asking people what they like and what they do not like about their work, data might be obtained which could permit a rating on degree of satisfaction or dissatisfaction with each meaning of work. Such ratings or scores could then be related to each other and to people's attitudes toward retirement.

RETIREMENT AND THE MEANING OF WORK

The Decision To Remain on the Job

As we progressed up the occupational and skill ladders, we found an increasing stress on the extra-economic meanings of work coupled with an increasing proportion of men who were unwilling to retire at the "normal" retirement age of 65 (Table 29). And within each of the groups studied we found that the individual workers who stressed the extra-economic meanings of work were also the ones who were least likely to want to retire at age 65. But to what extent are we justified in concluding that these workers were reluctant to retire because they had become dependent upon their jobs for more than the income it provided?

The question is a difficult one to answer in any precise fashion.

TABLE 29

PERCENTAGE OF MEN BY OCCUPATIONAL GROUP
WHO WANTED TO CONTINUE OR CON-
TINUED WORK PAST AGE 65

Occupational Group	Per Cent
Unskilled and semiskilled steelworkers....	32
Coal-miners............................	42*
Skilled craftsmen......................	49†
Department-store salesmen..............	65
Physicians............................	67†

* This figure is probably somewhat higher than it should be when contrasted with the steelworker group. About half of the coal-miners studied were already over the optional retirement age of 60; therefore we might expect that many of the men who might have answered "No" to this question had already been selected out by retirement.

† These figures are minimal estimates, since an unknown number of men in each of these groups who were not now employed had remained at their jobs past 65. However, the figures for these groups represent the proportion of men over 65 currently employed.

We cannot overlook the fact that many of the men in all the groups studied could not afford to retire. Yet we found that over 40 per cent of the coal-miners and skilled craftsmen and over 70 per cent of the steelworkers, salesmen, and physicians who wanted to or did remain at their jobs past age 65 gave reasons other than "needed the income" for doing so. And we also found evidence to indicate that perhaps 10 per cent of the steelworkers, 25 per cent of the skilled craftsmen, 50 per cent of the salesmen, and probably an even greater proportion of the physicians who wanted to or did continue working probably could have afforded to retire at that age.[3]

3. We might argue that these respondents were merely giving "socially respectable" answers and that the real reason for their desire to continue was a need for the income which the job provided. The researchers felt that this may have been true in some cases, but they also felt that the reverse of this phenomenon also was observed (i.e., some respondents seemed to have been rationalizing deeper motives for wanting to remain at the job in terms of financial need). Perhaps the two tendencies canceled each other out in the summary statistics.

The Decision To Retire

The converse of our proposition that workers who have found the extra-economic meanings of work to be important in their lives would be reluctant to retire at an arbitrarily set age was that workers who have not found these satisfactions in their work careers would welcome the chance to leave their jobs for retirement. Supporting this, we found a decreasing proportion of men who wanted to retire at 65 in the higher status and skill groups where the extra-economic meanings of work were stressed most strongly. We found, too, that an overwhelming majority of men who stated that work was primarily a way of earning a living also wanted to retire at 65; if they did continue (or wanted to continue) at the job, they indicated that they did so because they "needed the income."

But there were some notable exceptions to our proposition— not all men who found extra-economic satisfactions in their jobs were unwilling to retire. A consideration of the two groups of retired men included in our study—steelworkers and skilled craftsmen—will give us some indication of the reasons why men reitre. Of the 50 retired steelworkers, 18 (36 per cent) regarded work as only a way of earning a living and either welcomed the chance to retire or would have welcomed it if they had had an adequate pension. Thirty-two (64 per cent) of this group had found other meanings in their work; of these, 22 indicated that they were forced to quit because of a compulsory retirement regulation which was in effect at the time they reached 65, 4 indicated they were forced to quit because they could not meet the company's physical requirements, and 6 indicated that they wanted to leave their jobs for retirement. Of the skilled craftsmen studied, a similar slight reversal of our hypothesis was observed. Twenty-seven (25 per cent) of the retired workers had stressed the extra-economic meanings of work; of these, only 10 indicated that they retired because they were "unable to work" (mostly because of physical disabilities) and 14 indicated that they welcomed retirement. We have seen, then, a small but important group of men who, contrary to our original expectations, welcomed retirement even though they had found meanings in their work in addition to that of "earning a living." Thus, we cannot categorically assume that, because a man's life may have become intimately bound up with the performance of his job, retirement may not hold a set of appeals for him which is capable of superseding or even replacing the satisfactions he got from his job. Instead we have to contrast the nature of the satisfactions obtained from work with the type of substitutes present in the retirement situation.

Retirement and the Meanings of Work

Retirement is one of the very few approved forms of unemployment which our society allows its male members. It comes at the end of a work career and is presented as a reward for a lifetime of toil. As a reward it may have a varying degree of appeal for the individual, ranging perhaps on one extreme from a form of "time off for good behavior" to the other extreme as a successful culmination of a lifetime of labor and a chance to make one's fondest dreams come true. The reality of the matter probably lies somewhere in between. But, in either event, it can be assumed to hold a powerful attraction for the workingman.

The job, on the other hand, was also seen to have a set of appeals for the worker. These were represented, first, by the income which it provided—income which not only gave him sustenance but also contributed to his sense of self-respect and was a prerequisite for many of the satisfactions which he got from life; and, second, by the satisfactions which the worker derived from the performance of the job itself. In this study we were trying to estimate the effect of these two different sets of appeals on the older worker. More specifically, we wanted to find out what factors would bind a worker to his job even though he might be able to afford retirement—factors which might be assumed as complicating his adjustment to retirement if he were required to leave his job.

In evaluating our findings, we must guard against two possible sorts of bias. First is the bias of overenthusiasm which might lead us to underestimate the iron necessity of work for the overwhelming majority of men in our society—a need which is not as yet alleviated by the average retirement pension. Certainly the plight of the older steelworker gave dramatic testimony to this point. But, having accepted the fact that men do and must work for gain, we are then inquiring into the consequences of having spent a major portion of one's adult life in the activity which society defines as a job. To what extent and in what manner has the older worker found that the activity which he entered into because of economic need has, over the years, become such an integral part of his life that he is now dependent upon it for more than income alone?

Our second possible source of bias might be termed the bias of special pleading. The temptation is strong to imply that, because the worker has found added significance in his job, depriving him of it through compulsory retirement—even with an adequate income—would represent a grave social injustice. *No such case can be made in any categorical fashion on the basis of our findings.* We have found workers in all groups who stressed the extra-economic meaning of work who indicated that they would welcome retirement or, having already retired, were satisfied with their lot. Nor can we assume that retirement need be an unsatisfactory experience for many of the workers who feared that they would be unable, or actually were unable, to replace in retirement the life-meanings and satisfactions which they had found in work. But, if we assume a growing tendency toward retirement, the problem becomes one of finding satisfactory substitutes for the work experience, bearing in mind the possibility that there may be in any occupational group (and probably more in the higher skill and status occupations) a hard core of workers for whom there can be no adequate substitute for the job.

IX

Retirement from Work to Play

As our technology has become more efficient, fewer workers have been needed to do the work of the country, even though standards of living were rising and people were consuming more goods and services. When the depression of the thirties brought unemployment, the older workers were discharged first, and the Social Security Act was passed to give these people an income. Then World War II brought full employment and kept older workers on the job but did not modify the expectation that had been built up especially in big business and industry and in government and civil service—the expectation of compulsory retirement at a fixed age, usually 65.

ADJUSTMENT TO RETIREMENT

Retirement is a new way of life. The elderly man who has filled his day with eight or ten hours of work must find new ways of living these eight or ten hours daily. His wife must also learn new living patterns, with her husband at home much more of the time. The person at retirement must learn to do without the things that his work has brought him; and his work has brought him more than his weekly or monthly pay.

For some people retirement is a goal toward which they have been working. It is the culmination of years of hope, sacrifice, and planning. For others it is a trap, a piece of bad luck for which they are unprepared. What retirement means to a person depends partly on what his work has meant to him. If he can get the satisfactions out of retirement that he formerly got out of work, or if he can get new and greater satisfactions in retirement than he got in his work, then retirement is a boon to him.

187

What does retirement mean in the life-cycle? Is it merely a narrow band of years coming at the end of a full life and ending in death, or is it a broad stretch of opportunity to enjoy one's self, to do things one always wanted to do?

In either case retirement is a new way of life and carries some problems with it. There are problems of leaving work—of finishing things off, of breaking off sharply or tapering off slowly, of deciding whether to look for another job or a part-time job. Then there are the greater problems of entering the new life. These problems consist of learning how to manage on a reduced income, how to use more leisure time, and how to get new satisfactions to replace the ones that went with work.

THE COST OF RETIREMENT

Today about one person in four over the age of 65 is employed. Very few of the women are employed. Less than half of the men are at work. But a number of retired people could be effective workers. Estimates of the number of retired people who are capable of doing productive work under present-day working conditions vary from about one and a half million to three million, from 12 to 25 per cent of the age group. All thirteen million persons over 65 are consumers. By 1975 there will be eighteen million people in this age bracket—all living on goods and services produced by the members of society who are at work. Our tremendous productivity makes this possible. But the cost is a real one. If more older people were productive, several advantages might be gained—older people themselves might live more comfortably, young people could be given more education before they commence work, people in the 20–65 age bracket might reduce their hours of work, or the whole society might have more goods and services to consume.

The economic cost of retirement to the nation will grow as the proportion of older people grows, unless we revise our retirement policies.

For the individual there is sure to be some cost to retirement, if only the loss of the income which he has been earning. In addition, most people get other satisfactions from their work, and retirement means the loss of these satisfactions unless they can find other ways of gaining similar satisfactions.

THE RIDDLE OF RETIREMENT

As the time comes when work is not a necessity for the whole of adult life, older people are most affected by the change in significance of work. The primary function of work as the means of securing income is beginning to lose its significance for older people. Less frequently does the veteran of forty years of work say, "I have to work to eat. How can a workingman retire?" A pension can answer that question for him. He has earned the opportunity to retire and to live for ten or fifteen years of comparatively good health free from work if he wants to.

If work had only the function of earning a living and this function was discharged for life by the age of 65, everyone should welcome retirement at that age. But we have seen that at least four other essential functions of life are included in work. If these functions and the satisfactions they bring are lost by retirement, then retirement is an undiluted tragedy for a man.

The problem of retirement is to secure the extra-economic values that work brings and to secure them through play or leisure-time activity. Can this problem be solved? Can play have the same functions as work? Can play provide the satisfactions to older people that they formerly got out of work?

In Western society, work is by cultural definition sharply set off as the enemy of pleasure, love, consumption of goods, and almost every sort of freedom. Work is a task defined and required of one by other people. This historical cultural definition of work, we have seen, is not valid for many of the workers who have told us what their work means to them. They have found other and more pleasurable meanings in their work.

Let us consider the extra-economic meanings of work and inquire whether leisure-time activity, play, or recreation also have similar meanings, and, if so, how the meanings of work can be realized in leisure.

Social Participation

Being with other people, making friends and having friendly relations with people, is one of the principal meanings of work to people in all the occupations we have studied. This function is also served by clubs, churches, recreation agencies, and a variety of formal and informal associations in the person's nonwork life. The pattern already exists; the problem is to fill the void created by loss of work associations in nonwork life.

Interesting Experiences and Creative Self-expression

Work is not intrinsically more satisfying than play as a source of meaningful experience. On the contrary, recreation offers more variety and more flexible opportunity for creative self-expression and interesting experience than work does. The person who makes a hobby of woodworking or pottery-making, or plays golf or bridge, "just for the fun of it," or travels or goes hunting or fishing, is getting the same values from his play as though he were doing work for the sheer enjoyment of the work itself.

Routinization of Life-Activity

Our studies of the significance of work in the lives of people underline for us the importance of an activity that fills the day, gives people something to do, and makes the time pass. Sheer passing of time seems to be an important value of work. Work is admirably designed to provide this value, since it usually requires orderly routines. Even the people who dislike their work as dangerous, unpleasant, or monotonous often recognize the value of the work routine to them and cannot imagine how they would fill the day if they were to retire.

Retired people work out a routine for themselves, reading the newspaper regularly, visiting the library every morning or at definite times, attending church, sitting in the park on pleasant days, working around the house in the morning, taking a walk downtown in the afternoon, going to a club or a tavern at regular hours. But many people have grown so accustomed to having their days organized about a job that they are ill prepared to create a new routine upon retirement.

Nevertheless, leisure-time activities can be organized and scheduled so as to fill the day and make the time pass happily. Play can be made to serve this function fully as well as work.

Source of Self-respect and the Respect of Others

In a work-centered society such as ours has been in the past, work is certainly more effective than play in providing self-respect and gaining the respect of others. It seems unlikely that the present generation of older people reared with work-centered attitudes can get much self-respect out of leisure-time activities. Most of them, if they are forced to retire, will maintain their own self-respect and the respect of others by their reputation as successful workers and their feeling that retirement is a reward for a well-spent lifetime of work.

Women, however, have mostly gained their self-respect and the respect of others through being good mothers and housekeepers and neighbors. Women who have not been employed will usually be able to draw on the sense of worth and social prestige as they grow older that they discovered in their middle years.

THE RISE OF LEISURE IN OUR SOCIETY

Thus we see that leisure activities can conceivably offer the extra-economic meanings and values which work has supplied to people. This is fortunate, because leisure is on the increase at all adult years. A good many people now work forty hours or less a week, which is only a little more than half of the average work week a hundred years ago.

A person born into the "economy of abundance" which arrived about 1920 is growing up in a period when the use of leisure time and the consumption of goods constitute the major problems of domestic society. A person born in the work-centered pre-1920 society is a kind of antediluvian. The older people of today have the ambiguous luck to have outlived the period when their work ideology was dominant, and so they must adjust, somehow, to comparatively early retirement with more leisure than they ever expected to have.

Meanwhile the meanings of play and of work have developed

in our culture to the point where the old dichotomy of work and play has become meaningless. Formerly, play was a rest from the burden of work, but, as work became less burdensome, the dividing line between work and play tended to disappear. Formerly, play was a privilege and work was a duty, but, as work became less necessary, play took on some of the aspects of duty, and again the dividing line tended to disappear.

A new problem of design for living now confronts modern man. How can he fit work and leisure-time activity together into a satisfying scheme of life, with the relative proportions of work and leisure varying as he passes from adolescence to adulthood to old age?

IMPORTANCE OF THE LEISURE ARTS

The task set for modern man by the shift from a work-centered society to an economy of abundance with increasing leisure is that of *learning the arts of leisure*. By learning these arts well, people can enjoy retirement more than they enjoyed work.

The extra-economic meanings of work can nearly all be discovered and realized more fully in leisure activities. Hence we may state a principle of *equivalence of work and play*. In our economy of abundance, where work is reduced in quantity and burdensomeness to a level where it is not physically unpleasant, many of the values of play can be achieved through work and of work through play.

In addition, play has the unique value of activity free from outer compulsion—something only rarely found in work. The promise of leisure, then, is to combine freedom from compulsion with the satisfactions formerly found in work.

If this secret is discovered by people, the problem of retirement will be solved, provided economic security is also generally achieved. That is, retirement from work will simply be the signal to increase and adapt one's play or leisure-time activity so as to get the satisfactions from play that were formerly obtained from work.

But it is hardly to be expected that many people who grew up in a work-centered society will be able to apply in their own lives the principle of equivalence of work and play. That they do not do so is demonstrated in a study we have recently made of older people in a small midwestern city. This community, which we have called Prairie City, contains about seven hundred people past the age of 65. A cross-sectional sample of one hundred of these people were studied intensively. Forty-one of the people were either employed or had been employed and were now retired and were in fairly good health. (Another thirteen were at work or had retired and had such poor health that their physical activity was considerably impaired.)

The forty-one people were divided into two groups, those who were still employed and those who were retired. If they were applying the principle of equivalence of work and play, the retired group should have more leisure-time activities and a higher rating on a scale of intensity and scope of leisure-time activity. Results of a systematic comparison of these two groups indicate that those who were still at work had a small but systematic superiority over the retired group in the intensity and scope of their leisure-time activity and also that the employed group had a high rating on personal adjustment. Thus it is clear that the retired group is not compensating for retirement by spending more time and energy at play.

Further light is shed on the problem of substituting play for work by studying several men in this sample who had retired for reasons other than health. This group of men had average adjustment scores and ratings much below the men who were still at work. However, the best-adjusted man of the group has a very active program of leisure-time occupations. He has remodeled his home and added a section to it. He builds radios. He and his wife travel to Florida in the winter. They are active in a social clique that does a great deal of mutual entertaining.

In contrast to this man is another of the same economic status who says, "I farmed for forty-five years, and I wish I were still doing it." He putters around with tools in a shop in his garage but complains, "I just don't have much to do any more at my age." He never goes to the movies, has dropped out of clubs and organizations, and says, "I just don't go many places any more."

The first man is substituting play for work quite satisfactorily. The second man has not done so. Studying the lives of seven of the men leads to the conclusion that only two of the seven have been able to find satisfaction in leisure activity which compensates for the satisfactions they lost when they retired from work.

This small and inadequate investigation suggests a conclusion that is borne out by our experience in questioning people about the meaning of retirement to them. Most Americans are not ready to apply the principle of equivalence of work and play in their lives. Most of them are not accomplished in the leisure arts.

Possibly the generation now passing through adulthood will know better how to replace their work with play when they come to retire. They will have given more of their adult life to the practice of the leisure arts and so will be more experienced and possibly more resourceful in making use of greater amounts of leisure when they retire.

The personal problem of retirement for the average person will be made easier if our society provides more facilities and greater assistance for older people to learn to enjoy the leisure arts. This may be done through adult education programs, through public and private recreation agencies, and through churches and clubs.

In general, the trend seems inexorably toward more leisure time during adulthood and more leisure time during old age. We shall have to adjust ourselves to this trend, as we have to other changes wrought by technology. It should be possible for us to make something really profitable for us all out of increased leisure, but the task is yet to be achieved.

Index

Alinsky, Saul, 84 n.
American Medical Association, 156
Attitudes toward retirement, 34–35,
85–95, 122–27, 164, 167–69; anxieties,
95, 96; related to the meanings of
work, 140–41, 144; women workers
compared with men, 127–30

Bakke, E. W., 76 n.
Bituminous Coal Institute, 55 n.
Bower, Janet, vi, 180
Breckinridge, Elizabeth, v
British Isles, 56, 102
Bunyan, Paul, 31
Burgess, Ernest W., vi, 156 n.

Cavan, Ruth S., 156 n.
Chicago, 59, 102, 124, 132
Coal-miners: adjustments of, to job,
hazards, 64; age distribution of, 55;
attitudes of, toward union, 65, 66,
67; interview plan for, 55; job mobility of, 60; marital status of, 57;
nativity of, 56; rise in wages and
living standards of, 71, 72; sample
design for, 55; schooling of, 57; selection of coal-mining as a career
by, 58, 59, 79, 80, 81, 82; view of
job by 73, 74, 75
Coal-mining: assignment of easier jobs
to younger men in, 62; changes in
technology of, 53, 60, 61; effects of
mechanization in, 61, 62; hazards of,
62, 64; nonurban character of industry, 54; ownership of mines,
53; pensions in, 83, 85, 86; size of
mines, 53
Coleman, McAlester, 66 n.
Cook County, 156

Decision to continue work past age
65, 37, 142; comparison of groups
studied, 182–83
Decision to retire, 42–44, 143; comparison among groups studied, 184–
85

Equivalence of work and play, 192–94

Florida, 124, 193
Friedmann, Eugene, vi

Gerontological Society, v
Greeks, 18, 50
Gruen, Dolores Colen, vi, 157 n.

Hauser, Philip, vi
Havighurst, Robert J., vi n., 156 n.
Herrick, James B., 157
Hippocratic oath, 178
Hughes, Everett C., vi

Illinois, 53, 54, 55, 56, 156
Industrial worker prototype, 22–24
International Steelworkers' Union,
pension grievance steward, 33
Ireland, Ralph R., vi
Italy, 56, 59

Jaffe, A. J., 76 n.

Kerr, Clark, 76 n.

Language difficulty, 12, 18–19
Leisure: learning the art of, 192; rise
of, in our society, 191
Lewis, John L., 67, 84
Linton, Ralph, 5 n., 6 n.

Magarac, Joe, 31
Manley, Charles, vi
Meanings of work: association, 29–30,
70, 71, 111, 115, 139–40, 166, 173;
chance to be creative, 151; comparison among study groups, 173–74;
development of a philosophy of
work, 178; earning a living, 28, 68,
69, 105–7, 137, 150, 163–64, 166, 167;
earning a living as society's rationale for work, 139; economic compared with extra-economic, 137;
extra-economic, as describing the
part job plays in life of the individual, 139; feeling of usefulness,
70; intrinsic enjoyment, 118–19, 120;
meaningful life-experience, 140, 175–
76, 177; patterns typical of un-

195